TURTLE TALK

Voices For A Sustainable Future

Christopher Plant &Judith Plant

The New Catalyst Bioregional Series

NEW SOCIETY PUBLISHERS
Philadelphia, PA   Santa Cruz, CA
Lillooet, BC

Inquiries regarding requests to reprint all or part of *Turtle Talk: Thirteen Voices For an Ecological Future on Turtle Island* should be addressed to:
New Society Publishers,
4527 Springfield Avenue, Philadelphia PA, USA 19143,
or
P.O. Box 99, Lillooet B.C., Canada V0K 1V0.

Paperback ISBN USA 0-86571-186-0
Hardcover ISBN USA 0-86571-185-2
Paperback ISBN Canada 1-55092-001-4
Hardcover ISBN Canada 1-55092-000-6

Cover & inside graphics by Alison Lang.
Cover design by Barbara Hirshkowitz.
Back cover graphic from *NABC III Proceedings*.

Photographs:
George Watts, courtesy *Kahtou* magazine; John Seed &Marie Wilson, Anon; Susan Meeker-Lowry by David Albert; Murray Bookchin by Debbie Bookchin; others by Kip.

Book design and typesetting by *The New Catalyst/New Society Publishers*, Canada.

Printed in the United States of America on partially recycled paper by Whitehall Printing, Wheeling, Illinois.

To order directly from the publishers, add $1.75 to the price for the first copy, $.50 cents each additional. Send check or money order to:
New Society Publishers,
P.O. Box 582, Santa Cruz CA, USA 95061,
or
P.O. Box 99, Lillooet B.C., Canada V0K 1V0.

New Society Publishers is a project of the New Society Educational Foundation, a non-profit, tax-exempt public foundation. Opinions expressed in this book do not necessarily represent positions of the New Society Educational Foundation.

Turtle Talk is the first of *The New Catalyst*'s Bioregional Series and also issue No.17 of *The New Catalyst Quarterly*. For subscriptions to *The New Catalyst* and the Bioregional Series, write: P.O. Box 99, Lillooet B.C., Canada V0K 1V0.

Table of Contents

Acknowledgments

With the exception of the interview with George Watts—conducted by Suzanne Hare—all of the interviews presented in *Turtle Talk* were conducted by Judith and/or Christopher Plant.

The interview with Marie Wilson first appeared in *Healing The Wounds: The Promise of Ecofeminism*, edited by Judith Plant (New Society Publishers, 1989). All other interviews—except those with Susan Meeker-Lowry and Murray Bookchin—were previously published in *The New Catalyst* magazine between 1986 and 1990.

The New Catalyst Bioregional Series

The New Catalyst magazine is based in the dry interior of British Columbia, some 20 miles along a gravel road from the nearest town. From this rural setting in the Douglas fir and Ponderosa pine mountains just west of the coast range, a small community has been slowly building over the past decade or so, dedicated to trying to live an alternative to the Megamachine which threatens to destroy life on this planet. Part of this experiment, *The New Catalyst* has been published regularly by a tiny editorial collective since the fall of 1985, the product of home-generated electric power from a creek, as well as of much love and volunteer labor. Against the odds in the highly competitive world of magazine publishing, *The New Catalyst* has managed not only to survive, but to reach a steadily increasing readership scattered throughout North America—an achievement recognized by *The New Catalyst* becoming a finalist in the Utne Reader's Alternative Press Awards for 1989.

From the beginning, an important aim of *The New Catalyst* was to act as a catalyst among the diverse strands of the alternative movement—to break through the overly sharp dividing lines between environmentalists and aboriginal nations; peace activists and permaculturalists; feminists, food co-ops, city-reinhabitants and back-to-the- landers—to promote healthy dialogue among all these tendencies working for progressive change, for a new world. Early on, it became clear that the emerging bioregional movement was itself something of a catalyst and umbrella for these groups, too. Subsequently, but without announcing the fact, *The New Catalyst* became a bioregional journal for the north west, consciously attempting to draw together the local efforts of people engaged in both resistance and renewal from as far apart as northern British Columbia, Alberta and California, as well as the broader, more global thinking of key people from elsewhere in North America and around the world.

The New Catalyst's Bioregional Series builds upon the wealth of experience gained from people actually living and creating alternatives to global monoculture in their many diverse ways. It aims to inspire and stimulate the building of new, ecologically sustainable cultures in their myriad facets through presenting a broad spectrum of concerns ranging from how we view the world and act within it, through efforts at restoring damaged ecosystems or greening the cities, to the raising of a new and hopeful generation. The Bioregional Series is designed not for those content with merely saving what's left, but for those forward-looking folk with abundant energy for life, upon whom the future of Earth depends.

*

The New Catalyst magazine and the *Bioregional Series* are available at a substantial discount by subscription. Write for details to: *The New Catalyst*, P.O. Box 99, Lillooet, B.C. , Canada V0K 1V0

"These are wise and prophetic voices.... What makes them special is that they are people not merely thinking but doing, despite the weight of forces ranged against them—people who, it could be said, are sticking their necks out on behalf of all endangered species, including the human, including the living Earth itself. And it is the great lesson of the turtle, of course, that you can get ahead only when you stick your neck out."

FOREWORD
Kirkpatrick Sale

As it is told by some of the Lakota Sioux, the Great Originator made two worlds before S/he made this world: on the first world, the creaturers were bad and did not know how to live, so the Great Originator destroyed it with fire; and, on the second, the creatures were stupid and did not know how to live, so S/he destroyed it with water. And after the whole universe was under water, the Great Originator floated along on the surface, on top of a sacred pipe and a sacred pipe bag, carried by the waves this way and that for many eons.

At last, deciding to try one more time, the Great Originator reached into the pipe bag for some animals who would be able to swim down through all the water and find some mud with which to make the earth of a new world. First S/he sent the loon, but though the loon did its graceful dive and stayed under water for a very long time, it brought back nothing; "The water is too deep," it said. "I could not reach the bottom." Next S/he sent the otter, but though the otter used its powerful webbed feet to propel itself and stayed under for a very long time, it brought back nothing; "The water is too deep," it said. "I could not reach the bottom." Then S/he sent the beaver, but though the beaver used its great tail to force itself downward and stayed under for a very, very long time, it brought back nothing; "The water is too deep," it said. "I could not reach the bottom."

And so, finally, the Great Originator sent the turtle, who is very strong and able to live for a very long time, and has a heart so powerful that it keeps on beating after it is dead. The turtle swam down and stayed under the water for such a long time that the other animals feared it had drowned. Then, after a very, very, very long time—it may have been centuries—the turtle broke through the surface of the water, its shell and

vii

body covered with mud, mud in its feet and claws, and cried to the Great Originator, "I did it! I found the bottom, and here is your mud!"

Taking the turtle from the water, the Great Originator began scooping mud from its feet and crevices and, singing a song, S/he shaped the mud into a spot of dry land large enough for the four creatures to stand upon and rest. Then S/he took from the pipe bag two long wing feathers of the eagle, waved them over the plot of ground as S/he sang another song, and soon the land began to spread, and spread still farther, until it covered all the water but a few lakes and rivers and streams. Then the Great Originator opened the bag again and took out all the other animals and birds amd insects and fish and plants and trees, and with one clap of the hands, these all came alive. Lastly, S/he reached down into the earth and began to form the soil into the shapes of men and women, red earth and white earth and black earth and yellow earth, and with one more clap of the hands, all these came alive, too, each of them given speech and understanding and power.

Then the Great Originator said to the people, "The first world I made was bad, and the creatures on it were bad, so I burned it up. The second was bad, and the creatures stupid, so I drowned it. Now I have given you a third world, and if you learn how to live upon it with reverence and harmony, living in peace with each other and with all your brothers and sisters—the two-legged and the four- legged and the many-legged, the swimmers and the fliers and the crawlers, the plants and flowers and trees—then all will be well. But if you make this world bad, and ugly, and unhappy, then I will destroy this world, too. It's up to you."

And S/he named the land Turtle Island, for it was the turtle who provided the mud from which it was made, and S/he placed it atop the turtle so it would be forever a reminder for the people of the animal that carries its home upon its back throughout its life, and must protect and preserve its home because its home protects and preserves it.

And so it is that the land mass otherwise known as North America has come to be known as "Turtle Island," at least to some of the original cultures that survive today and some who have come to admire those cultures in recent years. It is a designation that defies the artificial political labels pasted on the map by legislatures entirely disregardful of geography, and tries to understand the continent more in terms of its basic realities, the natural features which truly demark and define the land. It is an idea that gives primacy, as seems right, to a remarkable testudinate order of adaptable, long-lived, and very tough land, marsh, and ocean animals, assigning them the sort of primacy that in other cultural myths is given to the large, bipedal primates who walk erect. And it is a concept that makes vividly clear what in these times has come to be called "ecological consciousness"—that is, the importance of the natural world and its protection and preservation as, in its necessary and inescapable way, our home.

Because of all these implications, the current movement known as bioregionalism has adopted the designation "Turtle Island" and made the turtle into what is in effect its totem animal: the turtle emblem appears on the official proceedings of the North American Bioregional Congresses that have taken place every other year since 1984, it is branded on to a chip of local wood that every participant in those congresses is given to wear on a necklace, it is printed on tee-shirts and newsletters and banners and books; and the clearinghouse center for the movement is called the Turtle Island Office. Having been part of that movement from the start, I have been especially delighted in that symbol because it has another and equally apt meaning in the culture from which I spring, as the symbol of the competitor in the race who is acknowledged to be slow and cumbersome and a little late off the mark, but also steady and sure and determined and persistent—and who eventually wins.

In the volume that follows, the multiple themes that the turtle image thus suggests, in its traditional sense and in its modern echoes, is evoked over and over. Some of the voices here who address these themes—who, it might be said, talk turtle—are conscious bioregionalists, with their special identification with that totem, but others have come to their perceptions from quite different, though obviously parallel, paths, some as diverse as anarchism and witchcraft, communalism and feminism, Buddhism and "monkey-wrenching." All together here, they offer a unique insight into what the human predicament is today, and why, into the true depths of the crisis of the industrial world and the gerry-built governments holding it together, and into what might be done to redirect society upon an organic, regenerative, sustainable, resuscitative, healthy course. It is, I would say, an astonishing assemblage of wisdom; you will not find anything like it anywhere today. Appropriate credit, and thanks, are due *The New Catalyst* staff that has found these people and gathered their words.

You will soon see the themes that these turtle-talkers evoke, and I hardly need to belabor them here. But I cannot refrain from underscoring what strike me as the most resonant and important among them: the essential task of getting in touch with nature, variously through a love of home and place, a ritual of witchcraft, an identification with the rainforest, an appreciation of non-human lifeforms everywhere; the essential need to identify with traditional peoples and regions, where the non-Western, non-industrial, non-civilized truths about satisfactory living lie; and the essential vision of the human as part of wilderness, still moving to primordial rhythms, able to restore and reinhabit natural habitats, knowing somewhere the links to the sacredness of life. And one more: the essential job of the present, of which each participant here is aware, of translating these ideas into a politics of the possible, a politics that somehow might have a chance of transforming us and our times so that we may build, as George Woodcock puts it, "the infrastructure of the new society within the old"—and doing so before it's too late.

These are wise and prophetic voices, then, but they are not disembodied; they are, if I may put it so, *rooted*, grounded in the real world of social action—writing, talking, organizing, restoring, challenging, sabotaging—as much as the real world of non-human nature. What makes them special is that they are people not merely thinking but doing, despite the weight of forces ranged against them—people who, it could be said, are sticking their necks out on behalf of all endangered species, including the human, including the living Earth itself. And it is the great lesson of the turtle, of course, that you can get ahead only when you stick your neck out.

Let the voices of the turtle be heard in the land. And then, as S/he said, it's up to you.

(From New York, Kirkpatrick Sale is author of Human Scale *and* Dwellers In The Land: The Bioregional Vision, *as well as having done a major study of the 1960s movement, entitled* SDS. *He is Secretary of the E.F.Schumacher Society and is also active in the North American Bioregional Congress.)*

"If we are to contribute genuinely toward saving the world, it seems that the only way forward is to follow the example of the turtle who, slow but steady, eventually wins the race."

1

Slow And Steady Saves The World: An Introduction

Christopher Plant

People told us it couldn't be done. Or else they said nothing—pregnant nothing—and we were left to guess that they thought we were crazy. After all, who in their right minds would believe that an alternative magazine could be established, and then prosper, in the remote interior mountains of British Columbia, with no electic power and no telephone, no radio or television, and the only work space squeezed into a corner of a bedroom? It seemed a recipe for failure, for magazine publishing is a highly competitive business at the best of times.

We did it, nonetheless. Although, in retrospect, it's hard not to agree with those folks who said we were crazy. The first issue of *The New Catalyst* appeared in the fall of 1985 after a tortuous learning process that, at times, seemed masochistic and without end.

We'd had the idea, at first, that we would simply type the articles on a Selectric typewriter, and put up with the amateurish look of it. But new friends made at a typesetting co-op in Vancouver convinced us that typesetting the paper might be within our budget if we were able to do all of the keying, providing them with all the material on diskettes. And it would certainly be the only way to make it look professional enough to succeed beyond the strictly limited confines of our friends and other devotees of the extreme fringe of alternative publishing. However, aside from a bare minimum of experience several years previously at university, none of us were really familiar with computers, to say nothing of owning one. What's more, we were broke; the four of us had just pitched in to scrape enough money together to buy the log cabin we were in, and we certainly weren't in a position to just go out and shop for a computer... Our dilemma was solved—as many more in coming months were to be—by a good friend who must have been prepared to see through the madness. So the first issue was typed on his Apple computer, twenty miles away, in town. We set up an elaborate shuttle system, some preparing and editing articles at home in the log cabin, while others drove to town to spend the day typing and printing them out; the next day, more articles would go off, while yesterday's were proofed and more prepared. Finally, two or three diskettes and some ten days or so later, it was all ready.

At this point, two of us climbed aboard our trusty, rusted, truck and drove the 220 miles to Vancouver. Because the typesetters used IBM-compatible computers, they couldn't use the disks directly. Someone came up with the idea of transmitting the data by modem. To do that, we had to have an Apple computer. Through more good luck, we were able to arrange with yet another friend to borrow his Apple, and cart it to the typesetters who would then perform the necessary miracles. Of course, there were the expected hitches that we came to associate with all dealings with computers, but, remarkably enough, it worked! In a matter of only several days, we were able to turn the truck around to wend our way back to do the paste-up, armed with highly professional-looking galleys. Now the challenge was to put it all together.

In the week that the typesetting trip had taken, others had been busy making frantic, last-minute page design decisions, and attempting to come up with a suitable "flag", or logo, for the front cover. Reunited, we installed ourselves at another, artist, friend's place in the valley and began pasting up the paper—a job we thought would take a day or two. It took almost a week, in fact, forcing our gracious hosts to run their diesel electricity generator for many more hours than they would other-wise have done. By this time, we had, of necessity, booked a printing date some time previously with a web press in Vancouver: the only real choice for printing a tabloid. As the days ground on by, we were faced with the gradually more awful prospect of perhaps not making the deadline. While we were later to get used to this adrenalin-packed prospect—the hors d'oeuvres, as it were, of the publishing diet—on this, our initiation, the idea of perhaps throwing into chaos our carefully wrought schedule threw added panic and pandemonium into the wearying crew.

Finally, late one night (another usual situation, we were later to find), and a zillion details later, it was all done! That is, the basic paste-up was complete, we just had to insert headlines, PMTs, other line-art and the line corrections: another visit to the typesetters. By now, there were merely hours left. Straining to remember everything, we boarded the trusty truck again for another five hour trip.

The rest, as they say, is history. We squeaked by. The typesetters dropped everything to get us to the press on time, burning more midnight oil in the process; in short, they were angels. The printers, too, were wonderful. And our Vancouver friends welcomed us in, put us up, and humored us as we awaited the pick-up time. On countless occasions, we've blessed our good fortune at having such good people to work with and care for us.

The big moment, of course, was something of an anti-climax. (Yet another thing we would slowly get used to, as we learned the brutal lessons of printing on an industrial web press whose tolerance for fineness and grace is low, at best.) The cover photo was darker and greyer and more opaque than we had anticipated; the whole thing was rather solemnly black and white; the design didn't *quite* work as well as we'd imagined.... But, yes, there it was: the final product! And if this issue didn't exactly save the world all by itself, the others surely would. You can't help being proud, even if your baby is a little bit ugly.

Little did we know, though, that having proudly picked up the fruits of our labor, *another* major round of work was just beginning. Now we had to distribute it. It took us another two or three days touting it around all the bookshops and health food stores we could think of in Vancouver. And then—after that long long drive yet again—we discovered the dubious joys of Canada Post's second class mail system. We'd begged and borrowed a few hundred names and adresses from various mailing lists and duly applied for our Second Class Mail Registration status. This they grant you with minimal trouble (provided you succumb to an examination at Canada Post headquarters!), explaining how you are to carefully sort all of your mail according to their Canadian postal code order, and bundle it up with elastics in deliverable quantities, then bag it up for the postal stations.... In other words, you do *all* their work for them, for the privilege of the discount. Well, since it made such a difference to our miniscule budget, we were certainly going to do it. But what a headache! Postal code order is like no other order in creation, defying mere mortal attempts at comprehension. From this first time on, it has been the single most dreaded feature of the entire operation, a real hair-puller, devouring every single nook and cranny of space in our entire house, and two or three peoples' devoted energy for two or three full days. It made us wonder. Maybe we *were* crazy??

*

The fossil fuels we'd burned getting the first issue out—12 to 1500 miles in a gas-guzzling, 1970 GM Suburban, not to mention the diesel fuel for generating power—and the overwhelming experience of the web press with its towering, whirring, deafening machinery eating up paper (and thus trees) at an alarming speed, raised questions in our minds as to how much this was truly a viable, bioregional operation. Especially since most parts of the process had been conducted away from home, and this was supposed to be a home-based business. In the following months and years, we set about the task of trying to improve things in this respect.

But we hardly had time to blink, it seemed, before it was time for Issue Number Two. So, despite the winter, and temperatures at times dropping to 20 degrees celsius below, the typing trip to town was done for this issue, too, as were the long trips to and from Vancouver to deliver and return the typesetting. But, by our third issue, with more advice from friends, we'd managed to find a few hundred dollars to buy an old portable Osborne computer—the one with the tiny, bright green screen—which would work for us *at home* since it could be hooked up using twelve volt power from a car battery. This was high technology, to be sure, and despite the operating conditions that we moderns would now regard as primitive, we revelled in the luxury of being able to prepare our text without the drive to town. It was our Paleo-technic period, as we dubbed it then: we would peer into the tiny green-ness, learning about cursors and formatting and copying and CP/M and all the rest, the manuscripts illuminated by candlelight deep into the night. Of course, we still had to drive to our ever-understanding neighbours to charge the batteries now and then, but this was just a minor inconvenience, relatively speaking.

By issue four or so, we realized that magazines could not be run without the use of a telephone at all. We had, moreover, begun to wear our neighbours' considerable and kindly patience thin. They owned a radiotelephone on which we conducted more business than was proper for good relations. More advice and more hundreds of dollars later, we became the proud owners of our own radiotelephone, entering the realm of instant—or almost instant, relatively speaking—communication with the outside world. Another great leap forward along the road of technological progress! Also by this time, we were mailing our diskettes to the typesetters and, within a mere week of waiting, could pick up the gleaming galleys in a vast manilla envelope from the post office in town. This cut the mileage, and our time in Vancouver, down to a welcome half. In the coming months, after some weeks of hammer flailing, we added an addition on to the cabin to act as an extra bedroom, giving us, at last, our own eight by twelve foot office. With tables and desks on every wall, and by adding shelves every several months or so, we somehow managed to accomodate the entire, burgeoning operation. *The New Catalyst* had come of age! When it came to paste-up time, we'd "clear the decks" and peer through the gloom at the layout sheets, illuminated still by propane lamps and candlelight.

Today, we regard our lot as quite superior to those days of yore. Through good fortune and the labors of our local electric geniuses, our cabin is now graced with electric power, generated by the creek that flows through the property. A marvelous, miniature, turgo wheel feeds power day and night to a bank of enormous batteries, giving us light and power enough to run a "real" computer. And, just lately, we've added a laser printer to our miniscule office, meaning that, at last, we're fully autonomous up until the printing stage. Wonder of wonders, we've also been able to profit from various computer gurus of the alternative scene, and now our accounts are no longer a Dickensian struggle with pencils and columnar pads, and the blessed mailing list now emerges in ready-to-bundle Canada Post lots... Hallelujah! Our most recent acquisition of publishing necessities, after straining our way through five years and sixteen or more issues, is a light table. Finally, we're getting equipped!

Nevertheless, we still operate in conditions that raise even a hardened eyebrow. It's fine for three quarters of the year: in addition to the publishing, we enjoy raising most of our own food, cutting our firewood, and participating in whatever community events we can, which range from hand-pulling the dreaded knapweed (to stop the Ministry of Forests spraying our watershed with Tordon), to communal potato fields and struggles to save the local forest. But in the winter months, we have to haul our water, doing without showers or running water. What's more, because the two inch water line that serves our turgo wheel is not buried (a major expense and engineering job), it freezes at seven degrees below, precisely. In and around that temperature, we have to pull the intake from the creek and rely on a noisy gas generator to back the system up. Needless to say, we push our luck at times, and lose the power overnight if a cold snap comes, the water frozen solid in the pipe. Ironically, it was winter time when we prepared the ecofeminism issue, and there we were, writing about the tendency of our society to always try to conquer nature, when the line froze in mid-operation. Ig-nominiously, we were forced to scramble up the hillside, blowtorch in hand, trying desperately to thaw it out, to overcome the laws of nature and force the precious water to flow once more, so we could add the final touches!

We're sometimes asked how we manage, being so cut off from the rest of the world, with no radio or television, or "proper" telephone. Although we'd boycott television, even if it were possible to receive the signal, we've often lusted after distant radiowaves in vain. But most of the time, we hardly miss that connection with the world—the daily news and hype—that seems so crucial when you're deep within it. After all, through the mail we regularly receive vast numbers of journals and magazines bringing all the news you'd ever need from around the world and, usually, you find out soon enough through the grapevine the important, world-shattering things of life. But exceptions do arise. For instance, it took us almost a week to hear about the San Fransisco earthquake in the fall of 1989. It so happened that we had been expecting a phone call from New Society Publishers' Santa Cruz office about an urgent matter. Instead, their Philadelphia office telephoned to say the call would not be coming as anticipated, because "it was just too crazy out there." With no further explanation offered (they must have thought that *everybody* knew), we were left to scratch our heads, imagining that the Santa Cruz office had been snowed under with an even larger than usual pre-Christmas rush of book orders. It was not until two or three days later that we saw, on the television at the local laundromat, that San Francisco and environs had been hit by a massive earthquake, leaving much of Santa Cruz destroyed!

Then, of course, there are the bizarre radiotelephone conversations, sometimes clear across the continent, that must surely titillate the local users greatly. Privacy is not possible with these devices, except on one side of the conversation at best, so everything can be heard by all who use the things within the local region. This is logging country, and the usual radiotelephone fare involves endless discussion of broken machinery and ordered parts during the day, and sad, separated family talk (along with some shenanagins) at night. The frequent talk of battles to save the wilderness, of ecofeminism and anarchism, and the less-than-subtle disparaging remarks directed at governments and the like by some of our correspondents have surely added spice and intrigue to many lives. We've wished on many occasions to be delivered from our radiotelephone fate, vainly seeking newer, brighter technologies, or even just a regular old telephone line to come our way. Once, not so long ago, we even asked the telephone company to quote us for extending the line the necessary five miles further along the road so we might be hooked up to civilization. Three men came out and spent the better part of a day estimating that, when all was said and done, it would cost us a mere $91,000 for the privilege. We told them we'd have three, and laughed together on the verandah....

*

From this tale of our experience with bioregional publishing, it's easy to appreciate why we feel that it's fitting for the symbol of the bioregional movement to be the turtle. For even in times of crisis, little happens quickly in the world of bioregional *practice*. Yet, seeing so clearly the urgency of the need for profound change in western society, the need—as the Worldwatch Institute has put it—for the 1990s to be the "turn-around decade", it is tempting to want to change the world too quickly. But it is that way that madness—and eco-fascism—lies. As Susan Griffin puts it, remembering Deena Metzger's words, "The world is on fire. We are all in danger. There is only time to move slowly. There is only time to love." If we are to contribute genuinely toward saving the world, it seems that the only way forward is to follow the example of the turtle who, slow but steady, eventually wins the race.

Our attraction to bioregionalism is that it is more than mere rhetoric or ideology: it proposes actually *living* the alternative, at the same time that we talk about it. And that, inevitably, takes time; time that, in the humdrum of the modern world, we are unaccustomed to taking. Part of the lesson that we have learned in making our particular contribution to the movement is this: that real change occurs very slowly; that, though we would perhaps like to be publishing more and better and bigger, our publishing endeavors are only a part of our whole life here. And, while what we publish may in fact contribute in a small way to turning others on, or "saving the world" in one way or another, what really has value may not be publishing at all. Rather, it may be the community we are gradually building in our valley, or the wider network of friendships beyond, or the experience we are gaining at becoming organic gardeners and reinhabitants. The times demand that we be accomplished generalists, that we actually value diversity in our everyday lives and, in practice, this means that we may not have the luxury to become the specialized publishers that a previous life might have imagined for us.

Despite this, however, we've wanted for some time now to produce even more focussed contributions to the bioregional literature—work that we hope will help save the world—and to publish them in a more durable, book form. Modest bioregional publishers that we are, the Bioregional Series is therefore a source of great excitement to us. It represents another, yet more unlikely, fruit for us: the result, in part, of a growing relationship clear across Turtle Island with New Society Publishers, a relationship forged in our work with the North American Bioregional Congress.

It is appropriate that Turtle Talk begins this series, as it is a collection of interviews, many of which appeared previously in the pages of *The New Catalyst*. Committed to reversing the impact of industrial society upon the Earth as much by example as by rhetoric, bioregional activists are working in their own life-places in a myriad of different ways to restore life once again to the living earth and people of this continent. *Turtle Talk* draws together some of the most inspiring voices from whose wisdom we can all learn in our efforts to create an ecologically sustainable future for Turtle Island. This collection sets some of the key directions for this crucial decade. It shows the diverse number of things you can do in your own lives, whether a town or country dweller, whether you have a propensity for the peace movement or permaculture, monkey- wrenching or writing.

Through these voices, the full breadth of the bioregional project is revealed. Gary Snyder, Peter Berg and Starhawk speak of the need to regenerate culture in its many particulars, not the least being our imagery and language, and our connection with the Earth. George Woodcock and Susan Griffin emphasize the importance of nonviolence in the process of building our new communities, and Caroline Estes' experience with consensus is an eloquent testimony of the value of learning new ways to do our collective business together—*social* sustainability. The need still to resist the ever-busy forces of destruction is clearly voiced by Dave Foreman, with John Seed adding examples from Australia's experience as well as speaking for the perspective known as "deep ecology." Marie Wilson and George Watts provide timely insights into how native people view the world, and how non-native people might best proceed in continuing to build alliances with them. From the east coast, Susan Meeker-Lowry clues us in to bioregional economics, and from the west, Freeman House shares his hard-won experience of being a reinhabitant: restoring a salmon run in the Mattole Valley. Finally, Murray Bookchin advocates a truly decentralized politics that would unite the city and the country in an authentically democratic future, a future of peace with nature and one another. Throughout, certain themes recur: the need to rebuild our communities and cultures; the importance of nonviolence and a participatory politics; and the crucial value of our relations—with each other, across ethnic groups, and with the Earth.

Of course, not all the contributors to *Turtle Talk* agree all of the time, and that's partly what makes the collection interesting. But whether it's a question of valuing utopia or not, or seeing the Earth as mother or not, or differing over the particular definition of nonviolence, the overall substance seems not to be at issue. At the end of the day, these voices leave you to decide upon the details.

In the final analysis, it is the diversity of approaches represented in Turtle Talk that is most appealing. Here, at last, there is recognition by key thinkers and activists in the movement that they hold just one straw of the truth, and that the way to prevent that truth from being broken is for the straws to be combined in a strong whole. Unexpectedly perhaps, it is Dave Foreman who stresses this: "If diversity is good for an ecosystem, it is good for a social movement, as well." However we try to move forward, to play our part in saving the planet, at least one or more of the voices presented here in *Turtle Talk* will resonate with you, and help along the way.

Turtle Talk is the voice of a movement in all its variety, an introduction to the full breadth of the bioregional view. Subsequent issues of the Bioregional Series will explore different aspects of this movement of so much promise in more and fuller depth. We hope you will enjoy them all!

"What we are saying is: regenerate culture! Grow back knowledges that are fundamental to being more at home in your language. Be more at home in your self."

2

Regenerate Culture!
Gary Snyder

*F*aced with the declining ability of the Earth to support life and the possible extinction of our own species, bioregionalists have long realized that a key part of our response to this crisis must be constructive, re-envisioning our relations with nature, repairing—wherever possible—the damage done to natural systems, and recreating human cultures capable of flourishing in an ecologically sustainable manner through time. While the progeny of a technological era is more than capable of tinkering effectively with technical matters, its expertise in cultural affairs is sorely lacking. Re-making ecological cultures involves, in part, re-working our language and our imagery—the provenance of poets and artists.

Gary Snyder is one of the west coast's best-known poets. Since the 1960s, his work—both prose and poetry—has inspired people to revalue their relations with nature. A long-time student of Zen Buddhism, Snyder celebrates the beauty and diversity of the natural world, and urges that we re-create local cultures that are firmly rooted in local places. As an early proponent of bioregional ideas, Snyder lives the lifestyle he promotes, and is perhaps best known for his cryptic proposal, "Don't move!" For North Americans especially, such advice, if heeded, would represent the first radical step along the path to a bioregional future.

The New Catalyst: *What is the origin of bioregionalism?*

Gary Snyder: I don't know where the term bioregionalism first came from. But the movement probably has its origins in the gradual expansion of the power of the city in European culture—at the *expense* of sustainable, local, small cultures. These local cultures, which usually have their own languages or dialects and their own traditions, have always resisted being swept into somebody else's urbanized mainstream in which they would come out second, both economically and culturally.

It's all part of the centralized state. Without even knowing quite why they must, except out of a spirit of sheer survival, small cultures like the Cornish, the Bretons, the Welsh, the Irish, the Scots—just to give a few examples in Western Europe—have tried to hang on through the centuries by the skin of their teeth, tried to maintain some of their identity.

These people are not only arguing for cultural authenticity and the right to exist, but also for the maintenance of the skills and practices that belong with local economies and that enable them to operate in a sustainable manner, via their own specialized, local knowledges, over the centuries.

From one angle, then, bioregionalism stands for the *de*-centralization of, the critique of, the state.

TNC: *Bioregionalism has both a political and cultural component. Can you elaborate on these two aspects of the movement?*

Gary Snyder: The aim of bioregionalism is to help our human cultural, political and social structures harmonize with natural systems. Human systems should be informed by, be aware of, be corrected by, natural systems.

Thus, the political side of bioregionalism, for starters, is recognizing that there are real boundaries in the real world which are far more appropriate than arbitrary political boundaries. And that this is just one step in learning where we really are and how a place works. Learning "how it all works" is an enormous exercise, because we are not taught to think in terms of systems, of society or of nature.

Then to speak of culture in the anthropological sense—and the Marxists would like this—a culture is profoundly shaped by its economy, its mode of production. The mode of production is enormously shaped by the materials. The materials here in Ish Nation are cedar, and salt water, and rain and clouds and lots of fresh water—fifty inches of rain a year, and up; extraordinarily high biomass. That helps shape the culture. It's no accident that North West Coast people spoke in so many ways, and made so many metaphors with salmon and with killer whale, and used as the primary mode of artistic expression the finest wood-working tree in the region: the western red cedar. So that's where you see the systems of the place literally stepping forward into the art and style of the culture. An inevitable intersection.

There are two projects afoot here. One project is to learn our natural system, learn our region, to such a degree that we can be sensitive across the centuries and boundaries of cultures. We should know what the life-cycle of salmon is, or what grows well here, but also become sensitive to what kinds of songs you might sing if you thought like a salmon. That's the learning that brings the place visibly into culture, into culture now moving from anthopological culture into aesthetic culture.

Continuing a dialogue between cosmopolitanism and the matter of being deeply local is crucial. To be merely cosmopolitan, merely international is not interesting. Because it tends ultimately towards monoculture, TV culture. Or it tends towards bureaucratic ideology: one set of ideas. So the check that is imposed upon the tendency toward centralization is the actual diversity of the world.

"The bioregional undertaking is to learn our region; to stay here and be at home in it; and to take responsibility for it, and treat it right."

TNC: *Could you say, then, that bioregionalism is an actualization of ecological principles?*

Gary Snyder: It is an *effort* to actualize ecological principles. But we're a long way from it. It's the effort also of social ecology, as Murray Bookchin defines it: to bring ecological principles, in so far as they are appropriate, into human social, political and economic events.

People have old ways of talking about these things. As they have "You are what you eat." There are maize- growing places, with hot summers and well-drained soils. So there are people who eat maize; and they have corn-goddess dances. There are people who eat rice; and they have rice-planting songs and birth goddesses who look like a sheaf of rice! And I suppose in Scotland, they have oatmeal goddesses! Some of our most fundamental lore is around exactly those kinds of specifics. And it need not make you narrow, or parochial.

The bioregional undertaking, for us here and now, is to learn our region; to declare that we are going to stay here and be at home in it; and to declare that we're going to take responsibility for it, and treat it right. And then to take pleasure in that and find what poems and songs, what art forms, what drama, what operas we can come up with—and what Prime Ministers!

The Chinese started writing nature poetry about 500 A.D. Now they had been a literate culture for a thousand years by this time. They did not write nature poetry for the first thousand years of literacy. But from 500 A.D. to about 1500 A.D.—a thousand years—they wrote an excellent body of nature poetry. In doing so, they gradually covered the whole landscape. There are poems about different mountain ranges, different watersheds, different tide-rips, different scenes, different islands, different conditions, different weather—wild geese doing this, and wild geese doing that. They covered it, you see. Now we've got a thousand years of poetry ahead of us just expressing North America!

An old place-based culture has a lore, a body of literature, songs, a kind of weaving, sculpture, a design on pots, that speak in subtle ways about the land. It comes back to us: like a haiku comes back to Japanese people. When they look at the bush clover with the full moon shining on it, they not only see the bush clover with the moon shining on it, but they hear a haiku of Basho's:

> Me and the wandering girls
> sleeping side by side
> in the same inn,
> the full moon on the bush clover.

Culture becomes interwoven with the natural landscape.

TNC: *If we are to reinhabit the world, how can we re-familiarize ourselves with language in the same sense that we would familiarize ourselves with the world?*

Gary Snyder: You could study the historical sources of the words. For English-speakers in the western hemisphere, we are ignorant about a lot in our language because we are now very far removed from the place where the language took its present form. So people do not know the meanings of their names. What does your name mean? (Gary means "spear" in Celtic.) Many people don't know their names. Similarly, Californians live on Loma Linda Land. Ninety percent of them don't know that "Loma Linda" means beautiful soil.

What we are saying is: regenerate culture! Grow back knowledges that are fundamental to being more at home in your language. Be more at home in your self.

TNC: *Can you speak a little more about regenerating culture as regenerating community?*

Gary Snyder: Well, regenerating any kind of culture helps regenerate community, and the other way round. It's mutual. Sometimes people become interested in family history. It grounds you in the world, in organic evolution, in the fact of having ancestors, the fact of belonging to the soil. It has a very conservative side to it: composting. Or recycling. Not losing entire track of old nutrients, but bringing old nutrients back into our language. Instead of simply continually taking off the top level, going down deeper and getting some of the stuff that's buried below the surface, that isn't used much. Understanding it that way, then you don't say, "Oh that's cultured, that's élite." You say, "that's just good fertilizer."

But all this could easily be taken as a simple return to cultural orthodoxy, or personal or regional parochialism. Those tendencies are dangerous, to beware of. It's this side of cultural regeneration, and bioregionalism, that makes sharp urban leftist socialists leery of it. Is this going to be a move toward re-building some new kind of Third Reich mentality? Here's "a people...." Hitler used a lot of the archetypes of cultural regeneration very successfully, and really turned many Germans on to a visionary sense of their own past and a phoney destiny. We're steering in very subtle waters here, and you have to be psychologically, historically and anthropologically precise about what you're doing.

"We are doing not street theatre, but mountain, river, and field theatre. We present a larger vision than most people have been willing to permit themselves."

This is why Buddhism is very important, and why understanding archaic cultures is also valuable. If you keep in touch with the Buddhist or Taoist insight, you're constantly reminded that, no matter what your cultural regenerative exercises are, they're not in the direction of revalidating hierarchy, or revalidating structures of dominance, or reconstructing the state. We are anarchists; we must never forget that. And the proof of anarchism is self-government. Without hierarchy.

So this is an anarchist exercise, as foretold by Kropotkin in *Mutual Aid* and as described, in contemporary terms, by Murray Bookchin in *The Ecology of Freedom*, in which we try to realize the true meanings of being local, and having a culture, without letting it pull us back into centralized hierarchical forms—which is where the Right wing wants to go with it all.

The most important Buddhist point is that human nature is empty, and that we are each personally not a simple ego but a system. Each of us is a system, of many selves, many memories, of many desires, many intentions, many lovers, many futures. and in understanding ourselves to be systems, we understand that there is no hierarchy of dominance in ourselves, either. The daily ego as chief is demoted to publicity officer. Realizing the arbitrariness of our several egos makes it possible not to wish to constitute an external version of authority.

TNC: *Many people would ask what the actual possibilities of the bioregional movement are in the "real world?"*

Gary Snyder: The actual possibility in the real world at the moment is as visionary social theatre. We are doing not street theatre, but mountain, river, and field theatre. We present a larger vision than most people have been willing to permit themselves. Our project is theatrical and imaginative at the moment, but ultimately very pragmatic as it moves down the line. And, as arts always are, just a little bit ahead of its time.

TNC: *In that visionary theatre, I assume we're coming up with images and forms that run counter to the prevailing images. What kind of counter-images and counter- forms would stir us up enough?*

Gary Snyder: The image of organism. The imagery of a marvellous complexity, working on many levels, in pathways too delicate to be grasped, and doing this in a totally uncentralized way. No center. No visible source of authority. It's potent. It counters the image of power as formed from a center.

" ...you have people who say, "I'm not going to move." That's where it gets new. People say, "I'm going to stay here, and you can count on me being here 20 years from now." What that immediately does is make a politically-empowered community possible."

A Buddhist image for this is the Jewelled Net of Indra. It's a way of describing the totality of phenomena. You imagine the world and all its beings as a three dimensional net of clear-crystal beads. At all points in the structure, all beads reflect all other beads. They all appear, each one of them, to contain the whole net. Indeed, if you put a dot on one bead, every bead in the net shows the dot. This is one of many images that people in the past have come up with in trying to describe the realism of interconnection.

There's also the idea of "mosaic." Take a map of North America—a colored vegetation map, such as exists. Look at that instead of looking at a political map with its bunch of lines, where Canada is pink and America is green. It's a mosaic of specific plant zones right up against each other. From tall grass prairie, to short grass prairie, to high sage. And west coast conifers blending into California oaks and grasses, blending into southwestern desert. That's the *real* map of the world.

We could also describe much of this as trying to bring the insights of much of science finally into our myth mind, into our feeling, to grasp the world as in many ways we know the world to be.

TNC: *So what might the bioregional movement best do right now?*

Gary Snyder: It's an educational exercise, first of all. Next, when you really get down to brass tacks, what it really means is that you have people who say, "I'm not going to move." That's where it gets new. People say, "I'm going to stay here, and you can count on me being here 20 years from now." What that immediately does is make a politically-empowered community possible. Bioregionalism has this concrete base that it builds from: human beings that live in place together for the long run. In North America that's a new thing!

Human beings who are planning on living together in the same place will wish to include the non-human in their sense of community. This also is new, to say our community does not end at the human boundaries; we are in a community with certain trees, plants, birds, animals. The conversation is with the whole thing. That's community political life.

"Bioregionalism is, from a Marxist standpoint, the entry of place into the dialectic of history."

The next step might be that you have an issue, and you testify at a hearing. You say: I speak as a local, a local who is committed to being here the rest of my life, and who fully expects my children and my grandchildren to be living here. Consequently, my view of the issue is a long-range view, and I request that you have a long-range view in mind. I'm not here to talk about a 20 year logging plan. I'm here to talk about a 500 year logging plan. Does your logging plan address 500 years? If not, you are not meeting your responsibility to local people.

Another person by this time takes the stand, from your same group, and says, "I'm a member of this community who also intends to live here in the long run, and one of my friends, Douglas fir, can't be here tonight. So I'm speaking for Douglas fir. That point of view has come to me by spending time out in the hills, and walking with the trees, and sitting underneath the trees, and seeing how it seems with them." Then speak a sensitive and ecologically-sound long-range position from the standpoint of the tree side of the community. We've done this in northern California; in particular a character who always calls himself "Ponderosa Pine." You can see how it goes from there. It's so simple. Such common sense. And so easily grasped by children.

It throws light on a more complicated political argument: an intelligent socialist-capitalist, class-structure- history dialogue. Bioregionalism is, from a Marxist standpoint, the entry of place into the dialectic of history. We are no longer simply talking about class. We're also talking about place. Marx missed that. His presumption was that the vanguard would be the industrial proletariat, that agriculturalists would become a variety of the revolutionary proletariat working on the land, and that local culture and sense of place were irrelevant and outmoded. But we now know, from science if you like, that locality will never be outmoded. Plants grow specifically to place.

You can over-ride the specifics of a plant's needs by fossil fuel inputs and by fertilizers. You can make an area do what it doesn't want to do by hitting it hard with a lot of herbicide and cultivation and so forth. Those all require subsidies from the fossil fuel economy.

Sustainable agriculture—bioregional agriculture—becomes sensitive and locally based. The cultivars that do well in a spot are the appropriate plants to grow there. The knowledge of how to grow those plants is the knowledge that is handed down through the people. It is very difficult to teach it in books; you have to grow up with it.

"The wilderness is *more* for our not having been part of it. We can see it as a model for ourselves: wild society! Bioregional and Wild!"

3

Bioregional And Wild!
A New Cultural Image...

Peter Berg

What do ecology, nation states, wilderness, and a new breed of urban settler have in common? Through the eyes of bioregional agent provocateur, Peter Berg, of San Francisco's Planet Drum Foundation, they are all elements of an emerging human consciousness, a transformation of society crucial for the continued survival of the planet.

Peter Berg and the Planet Drum Foundation have been key instigators of the bioregional movement from the beginning. From roots in the urban hippie days of Haight-Ashbury, when Peter was with the San Francisco Mime Troupe and was a "Digger" providing free food to the street people, he, his partner Judy Goldhaft, and a bevy of artistic- cultural-intellectual friends have evolved the bioregional philosophy from seed to flowering plant. Activists as well as ideas people, they have published Raise The Stakes, a bioregional journal, since 1981, have staged city-wide events, and—among other things—have torn up half the sidewalk outside their house and office and replanted it with native species as a personal demonstration of their commitment to greening the city—Planet Drum's latest and most concerted campaign.

The New Catalyst: *You were one of the originators of the bioregional concept over a decade ago, and the movement has come a long way since then. Where do you think it's heading in this next phase, the 1990s?*

Peter Berg: Probably in a number of different cultural and social and political directions, but the ones that interest *me* most are those that have to do with human consciousness in general.

One of the things that inspired me to try to conceive of an alternative to nation states, for example, in bioregions, was that, in the United States, environmentalism effectively came to an end as a broad *volunteer* movement with the creation of the Environmental Protection Agency in the early 70s. After that, environmentalism has only lingered on as a branch of the legal profession, whose primary job now is to bring injunctions, suits, etecetera—to prevent things from happening. But the pro-active element of "what should we do instead?" was obviously not going to be provided by environmentalism, but by ecology.

TNC: *How would you make that distinction?*

Peter Berg: Ecology is the interaction of all natural systems and beings in the planetary biosphere, whereas environment is really a view of what's around us, in a fairly narrow perspective. The best illustration of it might be that someone might say to you, "Don't step on the environment!"—as though you're not part of it. But, from an ecological perspective, human beings are part of living processes.

What happened at the 1972 Environment Conference in Stockholm, sponsored by the U.N., was that maybe 10,000 people showed up who didn't have any place to go forward. Because the United Nations, it turns out, is a forum for the *world*, and one could define "world" as the collision of national interests—as what makes the "world" as in World War I or World War II. But "planet" is very different from world. Planet is a living entity; human beings are part of it.

It was obvious then that it was going to become necessary to find a concept—a way of thinking about who we are, where we are, and what we're doing—that put us back into the planetary biosphere. For that reason, bioregion has proven to be a very useful concept to a lot of people. I see a concentrated effort on the part of progressives in general to assimilate this idea in all sorts of ways.

"Identify with that watershed, identify with that bioregion, identify with those native plants and animals!—Why? You don't even have to know why intellectually. It's where your allegiance lies."

TNC: *In what ways do you see it useful in the light of ecology as a broader frame of reference?*

Peter Berg: Because bioregion as a location is an ecological context. Who are you?—I am a person who lives in a place that contains other life, in ecosystems, and I am part of those processes; I am part of my bioregion. You can be part of your bioregion, but it's getting harder and harder to be a member of a nation state, in good faith, because the planetary biosphere doesn't have nation states.

TNC: *Let's talk about this bioregional, ecological consciousness. How does it differ fundamentally from the nation state consciousness?*

Peter Berg: Take the term "ecology" for a moment. The biological sciences are rather late developing in full bloom. Darwin is about a century after Newton. Physics is really well-developed before biology even gets its basic concepts going. And ecology is a late twentieth century word. It was Rachel Carson who put the word on the bookshelf with *Silent Spring*. She put it in peoples' hands, and she did it authoritatively, with the credentials of a scientist. This is 1962! Ecology is a very recent idea.

"Ecology is beginning to bend and reshape and transform every thought that we've had previously about human priorities. For politics, culture, society, human relationships."

The natural sciences and biology developed for a while like physics, in the sense that they were going to be used for industrial purposes (to take natural processes apart, disassemble them). But then, after *Silent Spring*, ecology started rolling in human consciousness. These ideas from the natural sciences started to come over into popular consciousness not as tools to disassemble nature, but to *see* it, to see its sanctity. So we hear the word "watershed" (which is just water basin terminology to a hydrologist). All of a sudden, when people say "watershed," they lower their voice a little bit. Or they say, "natural succession," realizing what a beautiful idea this is. And it's not human; it just exists out there. "Old-growth forest"—ooh, magical ideas! And becoming sacred to people. In bioregional workshops, I've said, learn these words like watershed and throw them at these scientists. Say, "Not in my watershed, you don't!" Say it like your body, or your home, or your family. Identify with that watershed, identify with that bioregion, identify with those native plants and animals!

Why? You don't even have to know why intellectually. It's where your allegiance lies. What is your homeland? Well, it's these plants and animals and natural systems that are in this life-place, in this bio-region. That's what it is. I feel this way about the Shasta bioregion [in northern California], by the way. I feel it is *my* home. And by knowing about it, by learning about it, I begin to authenticate my identity with it. By looking at native plants and animals, by regarding them, by paying attention to them, I'm putting on tree rings of identity.

Ecology as an idea has become that way too. It's not just a natural science concept. A *tsunami* of ecology is running through human consciousness. We're beginning to be aware: what are our connections? What am I really? What are my ties? Is there a future? Well, there's no future unless it's an ecological future: we know this deeply! Ecology is beginning to bend and reshape and transform every thought that we've had previously about human priorities. For politics, culture, society, human relationships.

So we're beginning to ask, what is the role of the nation state? It seems that it's a very destructive one from a biospheric point of view. Not only is it replaceable, it probably *must* be replaced by another view. Should my considerations be humanity? Or should they be human species in the biosphere? Probably human species in the biosphere. Should they be the workers of the world? No, the managers have to lose their chains, too. What is the purpose of growth in the economy? What is the purpose of progress? It seems that they're destructive purposes.

"...the greatest shared value for the necessary upcoming ecological era is wilderness. Because wilderness already embodies systems, designs, purposes that are workable, are demonstratably eco-energetic—efficient in terms of using energy and resources."

So sometimes I and other people—Thomas Berry, for example—will tell you that *he*'s the conservative. He's not cutting down the forests; radicals cut down forests. He's not doing open-pit mining; radicals do that. He's a real conservative, he wants to *conserve* the biosphere. We have to start selecting out ways to be with each other as human beings where our shared values are being part of the same species together in the biosphere.

My own feeling is that the greatest shared value for the necessary upcoming ecological era is wilderness. Because wilderness already embodies systems, designs, purposes that are workable, are demonstratably eco-energetic—efficient in terms of using energy and resources and so on. And they weren't designed by people.

TNC: *So you're proposing that this is the future- looking image, the hook on which we hang the next phase of history?*

Peter Berg: Definitely. Not only for protest activities—like preserving rainforests, for example—which are very important. But for these *pro-active* things to do. I think the image we want to conjure up is: what if it were wilderness, what would we do? Or, what if it was wilderness, how would it work? Some of the things about wilderness are very conservative. The way that plants and animals use resources is extraordinarily conservative. Lean and mean, if you like, not excessive. A lot of those images can come over into human affairs. But the reason why I think wilderness has such value for the pattern of values of the ecological era is that it is shareable, it is non-hierarchal. Wilderness has been outside the management of human consciousness.

In the industrial era, the image was material progress, transforming things, mutating things, changing their being, their shape, their chemistry, their nuclear components, changing everything about them! Whereas I think self- reliance, sustainability, climax, stages of succession—those are good images for the ecological era. And a lot of people can relate to them. They have a lot of lessons to teach about human interaction. Because what we have done in the last 250 to 300 years as a species on the planet is beyond the effects of the last ice age. We've destroyed more species, we've re-arranged more features of the Earth's surface, we've changed the atmosphere more, so we had better preserve what wilderness there is, and we had better attempt to restore as much as we can.

TNC: *How can human activities be redefined in the light of this new consciousness since our present mode of action is that mode of "progress"? How are we going to adapt?*

Peter Berg: Well one of the ways is in terms of political locatedness. I think the bioregion is going to continue to manifest itself in consciousness, even for those people for whom bioregion at this point is just an adjective. Pretty soon they're going to start saying the noun of it, and they're going to begin seeing that it is a life-place that they owe their allegiance to. So they're going to want political autonomy for bioregions.

There are some places on the planet where this already exists. In Europe, the boundaries of ethnic peoples can often be considered roughly bioregional. On the western side of the Penine Rise of the British Isles, for example, you run into Cornwall which is a bioregion, Wales which is a bioregion. The Bretons: it's obvious that they're very different from the rest of France.

As nation states become more desperate to control their situations, they impose more on the regions, bioregions, and ethnic peoples, and by so doing create in them a desire for a separate identity, and a feeling of deliberate repression of their values. In North America, this rule of foreign language and cultural domination was thrown down so heavily on the land, I think the places themselves are crying out. The places have more authority than the governments do!

"As cars begin to diminish, I would see a really cheery cultural prospect of tearing up streets, or at least tearing up half the street. And recreationally restoring creeks and springs in urban areas."

TNC: *The industrial state used the image of civilization. If we're to have a wilderness consciousness, I guess we'd be moving in the direction of having wild culture. What would that look like?*

Peter Berg: That's what I spend most of my time thinking about: wildness in people. Wild people—the people that we call primitive—actually have very ordered lives. The differences aren't in the *quantity* of what they do, but in the *quality* of what they do. They have deeper relationships with the things that they're involved with. Their cultural horizons are horizontal compared to how vertical ours are, where we always think it terms of ascendancy (get a better job, make more money, go up the ladder, get to the pinnacle of success—we have all these expressions). Whereas what wild people do is learn more about the horizon, more about what's out there, what's possible. "Success" would be more like filling in things you didn't have before, as skills, or experiences. Those are key differences. If they were magnified just a bit, we'd have a whole different society.

For example, right now, the idea of having a wild median strip that nothing could be built in, that was for wild plants and animals, run through an urban center is frightening to at least 95% of city-dwellers! But if you have more horizontal horizons, this is an addition, something to go for. Planet Drum's current Green City Program, thinking of how urban areas might be in bioregions, is a very horizontal idea. With median strips for wild habitat, and block-scale solar retrofitting of houses with maybe one little solar retrofitting shop per block, with secondary materials industries in neighborhoods. And small scale, so that you're not only collecting aluminum cans, you're making something out of them....

Wild is a good image for the city. Once automobiles are seen for the horrendous consumers of resources, time, energy, money that they represent now, for example, people will see that they are in fact enslaved by them, sort of the way that smokers see that they're enslaved by nicotine. As cars begin to diminish, I would see a really cheery cultural prospect of tearing up streets, or at least tearing up half the street. And recreationally restoring creeks and springs in urban areas. And in a horizontal, wild way, planting gardens, having a little grove of citrus trees, or peach trees.

"I think there's a new urban settler, a new urban person who belongs in the ecological era, who is much more conscious of resources, what they use, what they require, what they provide for themselves, what they do with their time...."

TNC: *What about the harder, more mundane question of how people would make a living?*

Peter Berg: Well, "live a making" is what we're looking for here. It doesn't take much to live. I mean we don't work for food! But outside of food, if you're cutting down on your expenditures, I think maybe Ivan Illich said that 25% of an automobile owner's salary goes to preserving that automobile? Take out the automobile and there's one quarter of your work day that you don't need!

I would also like to regain the notion of neighborhood culture. Before our urban areas got as run together as they are now, there used to be little villages. And eventually these villages just overlapped with each other. But they were little villages serving all the necessities that people require: you would be able to live simply within that one area and not have to travel. I can see regaining that as an image of urban dwelling. I think there's a new urban settler, a new urban person who belongs in the ecological era, who is much more conscious of resources, what they use, what they require, what they provide for themselves, what they do with their time....

TNC: *The city has always been a vacuum for resources from the hinterland, and it's been viewed by progressive people somewhat negatively. What I hear you doing is reidentifying the city in positive terms?*

Peter Berg: It has to happen. Because it has become the overwhelming habitat for human beings on the planet—fairly recently. Seventy five percent of North Americans now live in cities and towns of 25,000 or more. It's a growing trend and they're not going to go back in volume to the countryside. So they have to change. And, from a bioregional perspective, they also have to change because they're such a tremendous drain on bioregions. Living in the city—I'm an urbanite—I had to address the problem: how do you get cities off the bioregional back? And the way you do that is to have people in cities become bioregional and mindful of their connections to natural systems. I think things *are* changing rather quickly in the direction of a post-industrial era that I would call ecological.

TNC: *Do you see the idea of wilderness as having the power to liberate people?*

Peter Berg: When I think of the worst image of contemporary society, it's not necessarily one of the destruction, in ecological terms, that this society causes, but the control of the people it imposes. So that what makes me most indignant is the enslavement of potentially creative individuals to mass systems of information, or mass systems of political domination —satellite television, for example, or so-called "global" communication. Global doesn't mean that everybody talks to everybody; global means that *somebody* talks to everybody. Somebody controls "global", that's why that word is to be avoided in bioregional parlance.

For us to become liberated from such late-industrial forms of control, it seems to me that we need an image, a vision without which we cannot survive. That's what "freedom" was, beginning in the 18th century. Freedom suddenly became a flame. People would die for freedom. Think of the Paris Commune: people were so desperate to revise society in an egalitarian way that they seized part of Paris and said, "We will live or die to be this way." Well, I see us literally dying and not living if the depredations on the planet continue. And so a vision that is worth living for is what I'm hoping to get from wilderness.

"...our working together to discover our own wildness, the wild *homo sapiens* being within us, is very liberating, very exciting. It *is* the future from my point of view."

When I saw eight species of raptors in one valley the other day—hunting birds: hawks, bald eagles, a kite, a sparrow-hawk, altogether, obviously making a spring migration north; I saw about 50, but there were hundreds—I was looking at the survival of wildness. And it was such a positive image that I called a friend and said, "It's the best sign I've seen in months that it's still working out there, still working without us!" So I see those as hopeful images and as culturally supportive images.

I think our working together to discover our own wildness, the wild *homo sapiens* being within us, is very liberating, very exciting. It *is* the future from my point of view, and it's pivotal in terms of human civilization. We're making a swing from where we've been—assembling natural systems—to seeing them as possessing *more* for our not having been involved with them. The wilderness is *more* for our not having been part of it. We can see it as a model for ourselves: wild society! Bioregional and Wild!

(The Planet Drum Foundation publishes a journal, Raise The Stakes, *and serves as the main U.S. bookstore for the bioregional movement (in Canada, contact* The New Catalyst*). They can be reached at: P.O. Box 31251, San Francisco, Shasta Bioregion, CA 94131, USA.)*

"Witchcraft is one strand of feminist spirituality—the one I happen to come from. Witchcraft literally means bending and shaping the energy."

4

Bending The Energy: Spirituality, Politics And Culture

Starhawk

T*he task of creating ecologically sustainable cultures requires us both to resist the "power-over" paradigm and to put our energy into actually adapting our human ecology. The two are not, of course, separate. Much of the wisdom as to how we might best go about creating community, for example, has been gained in the contemporary struggles of resistance against the wars on people and on nature. But the spiritual values that might guide how we shape our new communities and cultures can also be found in the ancient pagan traditions of Europe which celebrated the seasons and natural cycles, the local plants and places of power, and which held an overall regard for the Earth as sacred.*

Long-time peace activist, psychologist, therapist, and writer, Starhawk— from San Francisco—is widely known throughout Turtle Island and Europe for her work on spirituality and politics, and especially for her use of Goddess imagery and her revaluing of "the craft," using ritual to build community. She is the author of Dreaming The Dark: Magic, Sex & Politics *(Boston, 1982) and* Truth Or Dare: Encounters With Power, Authority & Mystery *(Harper & Row, 1987), among other books. Her view of feminism is that it can be used to challenge all the relations of power in modern society. In this interview, she talks about how we can move closer to a future that is both spiritually and politically more in tune with the values of a new world.*

The New Catalyst: *In order to heal our relations with each other and with* *the natural world, you have said we need a vision of what the world would be like healthy. Could you talk about this vision?*

Starhawk: One of the things I did in *Truth or Dare: Encounters With Power, Authority and Mystery,* was to try to articulate some different principles for how to structure relationships and organizations that could help bring us to the vision of that world. The principles came out of an analysis of what's wrong with this world: looking at the questions of how we got into this mess, how did patriarchy develop, how did we, as human beings—who are actually part of the natural world oursel-ves—how did we create societies that are completely at odds with the natural world and which are likely to destroy us and the world along with it?

I wanted to look at the ways in which our whole emotional, psychic, cultural environment is toxic to us. They seem to me very linked with questions of power... power over and domination in the ways that we internalize power over. I trace this back to the development of that whole model of power which went along with patriarchy. I have come to see that patriarchy, authority, power over, obedience to authority—par-ticuluarly war and militarism—are the same thing, a whole construct of civilization. As they arose in the so-called great civilizations, they actual-ly warped or re-shaped the human personality around the needs of war and the needs of hierarchy.

Looking at the question of how you create a positive vision, you first have to ask how you undo the damage. One of the most effective ways to do this is by changing the structures of society. It's true that you can work on yourself and heal individuals. But in some ways it's like going on a juice fast and ridding yourself of toxics and then going back to Love Canal to live and work!

TNC: *So what kinds of structures do we need?*

Starhawk: The structures that create health are really pretty simple. First of all, there are structures and institutions where the inherent value of each individual or thing is central, where everything is valued for what it is, in and of itself, not in its relationship to some external factor like profitability. That's a spiritual value. It's a view of the world that comes out of the kinds of spirituality that have seen goddess, god, whatever you want to call it, being *immanent* in the world, not *outside* the world somewhere. Because if the world itself is sacred and we are each a sacred part of that, then we each have a value that goes beyond what can be measured and what can be counted. In groups and institutions that's just not an abstract idea. It means that decisions are made where each person's opinion and view and needs are taken into account, and heard, and—as much as is possible—are met. It means also that the economic structure values the needs of each person and supports everybody being able to develop themselves and live the kind of life that they want to live—that everybody has economic equal rights. There would be no category of people that could be written off. There's no room in this vision for men being more important than women, white people being more valuable than dark people—*everybody* is valuable.

"Looking at the question of how you create a positive vision, you first have to ask how you undo the damage. One of the most effective ways to do this is by changing the structures of society."

Another principle is the idea of real safety and protection. One of the ways that we become possessed by authority is in his guise as the conqueror, or defender against enemies. The way to undermine that is to literally establish some kind of real security. We've always identified security as more and more power over; the nuclear arms race is a great teacher about the limitations of that thinking.

So if you look at what *does* make people really secure it might mean the kind of culture which, for example, is like Switzerland where they haven't engaged in a war for over 500 years. They have a very strong defensive army and all the men are in it, but they do have other policies, too. Food is expensive there, but that's because the Swiss government supports the price of agricultural goods because they want to make sure that Swiss agriculture remains strong in case of a war. That's the kind of thinking about real security that we need, such that each region might be more self-sufficient, each individual might have more direct access to the means of sustaining their own lives.

Another principle is sustainability. We can't have security and we can't really value anything if we're destroying it. We need to give some thought to how to restructure our agriculture, our economic system, our social system, and our own groups, so that they can be sustained in the long run.

Finally, there's the principle which I think of as mystery: the idea that the world is not entirely knowable and controllable and measurable. Along with this goes a different attitude—that of wonder and excitement and surprise, rather than the attitude of "I know exactly what's going on and I know what to do about it, I know what the answers are." This is one way in which we've fallen down in forming political groups and spiritual groups. They tend to form around *answers* and then, of course, you can defend your answer against somebody else's answer and trash anybody who doesn't have the same answers. But when you have an attitude of mystery, then you've got to stay open to possibility, to say, well, this is where we see ourselves going right now, but we might be wrong.

TNC: *You have said that buying into the system is dismembering the Earth, that the Earth is the living body of the goddess. Given the reality of the society that we come from, how can we begin the process of dissociation from this destructive dependency?*

Starhawk: There are two things we can do. One is to create alternatives, to experiment, to create groups and organizations that are like laboratories for trying new ways of organizing ourselves, new ways of getting along, new approaches to questions.

The other thing we can do, which goes hand-in-hand with the first, is to mount really powerful, sustained resistance to the destruction. Oftentimes I have found that it's in mounting resistance and organizing, for example, to blockade nuclear weapons labs, that in the process we have created forms of organizing and decision-making, learning skills and tools which we can then take and use in our own lives.

When we began blockading, we began practicing and using consensus decision-making and forming affinity groups. What happened over the years was that the people who were involved in those actions started to say, "Why does it feel so good to go to jail? Why am I having more fun in jail than when I come home?" Of course, it was because of the people you were with, the way we were treating each other. So people began trying to live collectively, using the same kinds of decision-making processes and the same kind of sharing in their own lives as they would in an action.

TNC: *In an effort to gain human rights for women, feminism in its political action has become issue-oriented and specialized, which leads to burn-out. How can we avoid becoming lost in these details?*

Starhawk: I think part of what has burned so many women out is that we have to keep fighting for the same issues over and over again. We win victories over abortion and then suddenly they're going away and we have to struggle *again* for them. But I think there is, and always has been, within feminism a very radical critique of society. One wing of feminism has said, "Let us gain power within the system and equalize our power." Another wing has asked, "What's the point of having equal power in a system which is destroying the Earth?" What we need to do is use feminism as a tool for challenging *all* the relationships of power in society.

I see feminism as a process for asking questions, rather than a party line and a set of answers. You begin with your own experience and ways to communicate that, hear other peoples' experiences and ask, "What are the common threads and what are the differences, and what does this tell us about the structures of power?" This process can be applied to many things that seem on the surface to be separate issues—militarism, racism. But they aren't really separate issues, they're part of a whole system of power that needs to be challenged.

TNC: *What are the roots of feminist spirituality?*

Starhawk: Feminist spirituality is rooted in the process where women began asking themselves questions about their own spiritual experiences and found that there were things that they tended to have in common. Women have found that a lot of us have intense connections with nature, very powerful experiences in connection with love and human relationships and with our own sexuality, sometimes very powerful experiences in connection with art or with creativity, sometimes connected with pain, grief or loss. Out of that we can then begin to create ritual, liturgy, things that speak to that real experience, and intensify it and deepen it and allow us to share it, and sometimes create situations in which it's likely to be repeated.

"There are two things we can do. One is to create alternatives, to experiment, to create groups and organizations that are like laboratories for trying new ways of organizing ourselves.... The other is to mount really powerful, sustained resistance to the destruction."

Now there are also traditions and techniques for doing this. There are the old goddess traditions of western Europe—what we call witchcraft, shamanic traditions, tribal traditions—that are based on ritual and experience rather than on dogma. These traditions teach techniques for creating situations where that deep connection is likely to occur.

Feminist spirituality has drawn on some of these sources and has used them as sources for our own creativity. Witchcraft is one strand of feminist spirituality—the one I happen to come from. Witchcraft literally means bending and shaping the energy.

TNC: *How is witchcraft different from paganism?*

Starhawk: Paganism is a broader term than witchcraft. It's like saying Christian versus Southern Baptist. Pagan comes from a word which means countryside, and the people who lived in the countryside were the last to become Christianized. Before Christianity came into Europe, the witches were part of one or another kind of tribal or earth- tradition similiar to Native American traditions. Their religions celebrated the seasons and the cycles, the local plants, the powers of the places where people lived and the sacred connections with the Earth. The theologies centered around the cycles of birth, growth, death and renewal, and rebirth in nature and within the human community—as well as the way in which all of those are balanced.

TNC: *You belong to a coven and you once told a story about a ritual for the daughter of one of your group who was coming into puberty. Can you share that?*

Starhawk: For women, menstruation is one of the prime things that we don't have a positive ritual for in this culture. In fact, it's tremendously embarrassing. The one that we did for the daughter of the woman in the coven went like this.

We took both the mother and daughter to the beach and tied them together with a silver cord and they ran as far as the mother could run and, when she couldn't run any further, we cut the cord and the daughter ran on alone. Then we went back and we spent some time in the hot tub, 13 women, each telling the story of how it was that she became a woman. We gave presents. Gave her a robe which we had embroidered. We wanted this to be a women's mystery, just for women, but we also wanted her to have the experience of celebration by men. So we asked the men who were friends to prepare a feast. They prepared a wonderful potluck of red foods. In some ways it was healing for all of us; though we did it for her, we also did it for ourselves.

TNC: *How does your work relate to the Green movement?*

Starhawk: We share a lot of the same values with the Green movement. But my experience in Germany, where I have been several times and done a lot of workshops, is that the Green movement there would not define itself as a spiritual movement. The people who are involved in spirituality have green sympathies but are not very active in the Green Party. There is still a very deep split there between politics and spirituality which reflects their history with the Nazis, especially. They're scared, and not without good reason.

In North America, the Green movement is coming out of a kind of linking between a spiritual vision and a political vision that the direct action and peace movements and the feminist movement have been coming to for a long time. Here, spirituality may be more of an innate focus.

To me, the way spirituality and politics are linked is that if you have a spiritual vision that says that what we call spirit is immanent in the world, then that shapes your values, and your values shape your actions.

This is how you develop spirituality, through enacting what you value. Things like ritual and celebration are important tools that are available to us. They're great when they work, but they're not really what's central. What's central are the values and what you do about them.

At the same time, I think there are very important ways that spirituality and politics should *not* come together. You can't say, let's sit down and see what kind of spirituality we should have that will appeal to the vast majority of voters. It doesn't work that way. If you have a spiritual vision, then you have a responsibility to that vision. You act and you do it. I think there's a real danger in trying to tailor your spirituality to meet certain political ends and goals. It takes the mystery out of it.

"...the way spirituality and politics are linked is that if you have a spiritual vision that says that what we call spirit is immanent in the world, then that shapes your values, and your values shape your actions."

TNC: *Many revolutions have invariably ended up repeating the same process which we not very long ago separated ourselves from. How can we ensure that we are, indeed, involved in evolution and not revolution?*

Starhawk: By keeping firmly to that principle of the inherent value of every being. What has often happened in revolutions is that it's been thought that our group has more value than this other group, so let's purge them. For example, people in the deep ecology movement—which puts forth many principles that are really very close to what I've been saying—have said in print that the world population needs to be reduced; therefore let's not send aid to Africa because nature is taking its course. That's a horrifying statement. [Made by Dave Foreman, of *Earth First!*, when interviewed by Bill Devall, author of *Deep Ecology: Living As If Nature Mattered*, for *Simply Living*, an Australian magazine.] First of all, it's not nature taking its course. Anyone with any historical understanding knows that those famines have been produced by an economic system that doesn't allow people control over their own lives and decisions and lands, and exploits certain people for the advantage of other people.

Secondly, it's very dangerous to say world population must be reduced in a world in which some of the population has always been inherently more valued than others. Because then what we tend to do is just write off the rest, write off the Africans, write off the gay people, write off people who are not just like us. That's where we get out of a positive movement towards real change and back into another version of the same old stuff. If we're talking about reducing the human population, then we're talking about something that's going to come over the long term, gradually, out of those people's free choice when they really understand what's going on.

There are tried and true and effective ways of reducing population. What they are is feminism. When you have a society in which women begin to have more options in their lives, more education, more opportunities for other kinds of work, where you have more security and more safety for the lives of the children who actually exist, where you have economic systems where old people have security and support coming from the whole culture rather than just their immediate family, then people will voluntarily reduce their families. This is where the ecology movement needs to read up a bit on feminism.

There's a lot to be done right now and it's exciting work, and the important thing is that, whatever we're doing, to not approach it out of guilt, and doom and gloom, and despair. This is part of the pagan perspective on politics: that we don't have to be in it to suffer. That's doing *their* work for them! When we organize and take action, one of the principles should be that we treat each other well, for the way we treat each other in our groups is maybe as important—or perhaps *more* important—than anything we actually get done.

5

Mutual Aid:
The Seed Of The Alternative

George Woodcock

Violence is very much a part of the fabric of modern industrial society. As such, many social thinkers have been committed to examining why this is so, and what alternative, nonviolent social forms might be possible. The potential for such change is what inspires many bioregional ideas, with their accent on self-reliance, local control of local resources by local people, and the devolution of political power away from centers where its concentration has historically led to its abuse: the tyranny of one group over another, or of an alienated human population over the rest of nature.

George Woodcock, one of British Columbia's most prolific writers and critics, is known for his study of anarchism and his belief that, in its nonviolent, decentralist form, it represents the structure with the best chance of creating a participatory, peaceful society. He has also written widely on the arts, British Columbia's geography, its native peoples, and on communities such as the Doukhobours, as well as international figures like Mahatma Gandhi, the Indian proponent of nonviolence. In this interview, he talks about nonviolence, the structure of society, and the history of attempts to create alternatives, both at home and abroad.

The New Catalyst: *Nonviolence is very much a part of one strand of the anarchist tradition which has viewed humankind as naturally social and co-operative, rather than aggressive. What are the major assumptions and features of this tradition, and at what points does it most conflict with the assumptions of modern industrial society?*

George Woodcock: There has been a recurrent division among anarchists between those who advocate and—with growing rareness—practice violence, and those who reject violence on the grounds that, if it is directed against other human beings, it is a kind of power and no better than any other. What assault on another person's freedom could be more extreme than to kill him or her?

The peak of anarchist violence in propaganda and deed was during the late nineteenth century and it was largely an extreme manifestation of the romantic revolutionism of the age, with its cult of barricade heroism. But throughout that period there were thinkers who propounded what were really anarchist ideas of social organization and at the same time favoured nonviolent methods: William Godwin, Pierre-Joseph Proudhon, Leo Tolstoy, Gandhi. Interestingly, though Tolstoy avoided accepting the label of anarchist because in his time the more violent faction was in the ascendant, Gandhi did on several occasions call himself an anarchist, and there is no doubt that he was influenced considerably by the anarchist Peter Kropotkin, whose *Fields, Factories and Workshops* was one of the earliest pleas for industrial decentralization.

Social and industrial decentralization, in the sense of the dismantling of the power structure on all levels, is a logical development from the anarchist criticism of the state. Financial power and industrial power have always been seen as existing parallel to and interdependent with political power and, in one form or another, the anarchists have always advocated workers' control of factories and services, and the administration of industrial as well as social functions by those most directly involved. While there are some currents in modern industrial society that often seem to tend towards decentralization, particularly in the more sophisticated newer industries, the general trend is still towards a centralization of *control* even if not of *function*, whether it is a matter of the state control favored by communists and most socialists, or the corporate control represented by large national and multinational combines. Against the current reality of centralized control, the anarchist poses the federal model, in which autonomous undertakings loosely associate in the pursuit of common interests. Essentially, the anarchist believes that, given the broadest possible freedom to develop, people's natural tendency to co-operate will produce viable institutions, and that centralized authority, by discouraging voluntary urges, tends to eliminate natural social instincts. The impossibility of reconciling the two viewpoints means that anarchists have not only opposed right-wing authoritarian regimes but also the state-oriented tendencies within socialism.

TNC: *Today's trend toward greater and greater centralization of decision-making authority is being accompanied in many places by a movement for local control and the creation of self-governing communities, as structures that are not inherently as violent as the centralized state. What examples are there in history of similar movements, what became of them, and how do you see this current movement developing?*

George Woodcock: At certain periods, historical circumstances have favored the emergence and temporary flourishing of communities that tried to be self-contained and self-governing. In the early 19th century, a considerable number of Owenite and other utopian socialist communities appeared in North America; in England during World War II there was a tendency for pacifists to create small agrarian communities as an alternative to the war- based society around them; during the 1960s, when the idea of participatory democracy blossomed, there was another movement of intentional communities. Most of them died, some more quickly than others. The lesson seemed to be that a self-contained community within an unsympathetic society could not survive merely on the intention of its members to create such a community. The social vision was not in itself enough, and the communities that have survived are those, like the Hutterites, who have some transcending religious vision. The same applies to monastic communities. Paradoxically, by rejecting the values of this world, such communities create the disciplines that enable them to survive within it.

"...people are naturally inclined to meet their common needs by creating their own associations for practicing mutual aid. The state—especially the welfare state— erodes these natural manifestations of co-operation by replacing them with bureaucratic structures."

Otherwise, the successful libertarian social experiments have tended to be those of limited objectives, like co- operatives, credit unions, progressive schools, non- governmental organizations for foreign aid, and environmental action groups like Greenpeace. Some of these have developed into complex, multi-functional organizations like the Mondragon movement in the Spanish Basque country, which includes producer and consumer co-operatives, education, housing and retirement schemes, so that its thousands of members are virtually provided for from cradle to grave. One of the secrets of Mondragon's success may be that communal productive, consumer and social services are not accompanied by actual communal living; the individual and the family retain their privacy within the group.

TNC: *The nonviolent vision calls for the transformation of existing social institutions—a long- term aim—rather than immediate political revolution: a matching of ends and means. If this was true for Gandhi, do you think that it still holds true for us today, when radical social change is so urgently needed?*

George Woodcock: Nowadays many anarchist thinkers, like Colin Ward, Paul Goodman and I, have been turning away from the myth of the liberating revolution, realizing that revolutions in practice recreate authoritarian structures often worse than those that have preceded them, and we have developed a more pragmatic and evolutionary approach. We have gone back to Kropotkin's argument in *Mutual Aid* that people are naturally inclined to meet their common needs by creating their own associations for practicing mutual aid. The state—especially the welfare state—erodes these natural manifestations of co-operation by replacing them with bureaucratic structures. But the tendency towards mutual aid remains, and so, waiting to be reactivated, do many of the relationships on which it could build. It seems to us that anarchists today are better employed building the infrastructure of a new society within the old by creating or reviving mutual aid situations, and working with co-operative, environmentalist and anti-war movements in a constructive way, than in thinking in terms of revolution, which—as the examples of so many countries have recently shown—is likely to lead to new forms of dictatorship rather than to freedom and justice.

"Gandhi believed that the village should become the basis of a decentralized, non-militarist libertarian society stressing co-operation and community ownership—though largely individual cultivation—of the land."

TNC: *By reviving spinning as an activity he personally undertook, Gandhi was calling for the regeneration of cottage industry as the basis for nonviolent, local economies. Community land ownership was also a part of this scheme. How successful have these movements been in India, and how are they reflected today?*

George Woodcock: Gandhi's realism led him to be specific in his social programs, and when he promoted hand spinning he meant it as an activity, both practical and symbolic, directed at India's special needs as a country with a vast population, largely unemployed or under-employed, which needed labour-intensive solutions. Spinning thus became not merely a cottage industry; it was part of Gandhi's plan for village regeneration. Recognizing that 75% of the population of India lived in villages (a proportion little changed since his time) he believed that the village should become the basis of a decentralized, non-militarist libertarian society stressing co-operation and community ownership—though largely individual cultivation—of the land. During the struggle for liberation, Congress paid lip service to Gandhi's ideals. But when independence was won, the leaders in power, notably Nehru, set out to make India a centralized, industrialized and militarist nation state like the Britain from which Indians had struggled to be free. Thus Gandhi's hope of making India the model for a new kind of society to follow the end of colonialism was frustrated.

From this point Gandhism became a minor current in Indian life, occasionally coming to public attention, as in Vinoba Bhave's great land-gathering pilgrimages, but practiced only by small numbers of dedicated Gandhians in any sustained way. [Early on, Vinoba Bhave had been chosen by Gandhi to court arrest and make public statements opposing war.] However, the idea of village regeneration based on self-help and of self-governing agricultural communes persists. Among the most succesful manifestations has been the Sarva Seva movement, which took over apparently barren land donated to Vinoba Bhave and, by providing water and giving help over limited periods (usually three years) has settled thousands of *harijans* (once called untouchables) in prosperous villages, where the farmers have possession of the land so long as they or their descendants cultivate it, but are unable to sell it. Once a family ceases to cultivate its land, it is returned to the communal pool and is reassigned. In this way the old Indian evil of land falling into the hands of money lenders has been eliminated. Thus, on a small scale, Gandhi's ideas are being worked out in modern India, but a large-scale movement of village regeneration of the kind he hoped for has not materialized. Yet it seems the only hope for solving India's main problem: a vast pool of landless rural poor (roughly 300 million) who create urban problems as well by flooding into the city slums where neither work nor welfare awaits them. The hundreds of thousands of derelict villages must be turned into living, working communities to provide homes for the homeless and work for the workless if that problem is to be solved. Gandhi offered the only solution; it is India's tragedy that it was ignored by the men who acquired power at the time of liberation in 1947.

TNC: *Do you think that the examples from Gandhi's India are transferrable to North America?*

George Woodcock: I believe Gandhi's teachings of rural revitalization based on self-help have important lessons for all developing countries.

To us in Canada they offer the suggestion that, if the current trend towards corporate control of agriculture could be reversed, the countryside might once again sustain relatively large numbers of people in an economy integrating agriculture and other manual crafts. This would bring back into cultivation the considerable areas of marginal land that have been deserted but which could be adapted to intensive rather than extensive farming.

"Nonviolent movements may achieve only limited immediate objectives but often change the way a whole society sees itself, and do so without endangering freedom and imposing ruthless dictatorships."

TNC: *Nonviolent civil disobedience can be seen as the political strategy of the nonviolent view, and was practiced widely in Gandhi's India, by Martin Luther King and the American civil rights movements, and still today in the peace and environmental movements especially. Yet critics are quick to call the strategy naive and unrealistic. What have been the lasting accomplishments of civil disobedience as a strategy, and how would you respond to such a criticism?*

George Woodcock: Whenever I hear nonviolent civil disobedience criticized as naive and unrealistic, I find that for an answer I have to look no farther than the alternative. One can, indeed, by violent revolutionary action, bring a relatively quick end to a hated tyranny. But what does one have in its place? Another tyranny, with a different name. Because violence and power are linked irrevocably, and a violent revolution is a transfer of power. So that on the morrow of the revolution we are once again in the position of some being the ruled and some the rulers, and the people who are really interested in freedom are once again hunted down, by a secret police with a new name. All recent revolutions have followed this course, which is a consequence of the whole reactionary Leninist concept of the coup d'état by a party "representing" the proletariat which, in accordance with classic Marxist doctrine, establishes a temporary dictatorship that turns out to be permanent. Like other pacifists, I protested against the Vietnamese war because it was a war, not because I had any illusions about the Viet Cong, whose eventual triumph led to a totalitarian nightmare. Similarly, I expected nothing else from the Cuban or the Nicaraguan revolutions than what has happened: the steady erosion of freedoms of speech and writing, the elimination of democratic opposition, the consolidation of one-party rule imposed by physical force. Nonviolent movements may achieve only limited immediate objectives but often change the way a whole society sees itself, and do so without endangering freedom and imposing ruthless dictatorships. Who ever heard of a pacifist Mao, or Castro, or Ortega? It strikes me, I repeat, that the naive ones are those who expect violence in revolt to produce anything but violence in victory, or force to create anything but repression.

TNC: *Nonviolence, as an action strategy, is often accompanied by a utopian vision that provides inspiration for the kind of society toward which one is working. What examples are there in Canada's history—and British Columbia's in particular—of both the utopian visions, and the attempts to put them into practice?*

George Woodcock: I cannot speak for other proponents of nonviolence, but, as an anarchist, I have always been anti-utopian, believing that humankind, in its present unfree condition, cannot plan the lives of people in the future who—hopefully—will be more free. A utopian vision is an imposition on the future of the ideas of the present, but human beings can only form their institutions according to the realities of their particular times and places. Socialists, who usually have authoritarian minds, find no difficulty in making blueprints for their children. Anarchists consider it an arrogant imposition, so that though anarchists will offer tentative theories about how a free society may work, they have rarely written detailed plans of how it *will* work.

"The initiatives for change have to operate within the society's structure, not in isolation from it, and have to encourage the growth of tendencies that represent mutual aid and co-operation at the expense of the negative tendencies of political manipulation and bureaucratic control."

Hence I do not find it surprising that such utopian ventures as have been tried in Canada have for the most part failed to work out, or to have any appreciable influence. Perhaps the two most ambitious utopian undertakings in western Canada were the Finnish socialist community of Sointula on Malcolm Island near Alert Bay, and the Doukhobor community under Peter the Lordly Verigin in the Kootenays, both in the early years of the present century. The Sointula community lasted from 1901 to 1904 and, during that time, perhaps 2,000 people passed through, some staying only a few weeks. At no time were there more than 300 people in residence. The ideals with which the community began were well-considered; it fell down over the problem of translating general theories into the details of daily living, and over personality conflicts.

The Doukhobor community was even larger, and for years maintained a population of between five and six thousand people. In its earlier years, inspired by its first leader, Peter the Lordly, it reached a high level of productivity, with extensive communal farms and orchards, brick works, sawmills, jam factories, and so on. Most of all it was sustained by religious fervor. The schismatic tendencies of the Doukhobors, combined with poor leadership after Verigin's death in 1924 and the external circumstances of the Depression, brought about its collapse in the 1930s.

Such lessons—and almost every utopian community in history offers a similar example of failure—lead me again to the conclusion that society cannot be changed by setting up exemplary cells of perfect living that are detached from its main tendencies. The initiatives for change have to operate within the society's structure, not in isolation from it, and have to encourage the growth of tendencies that represent mutual aid and co-operation at the expense of the negative tendencies of political manipulation and bureaucratic control.

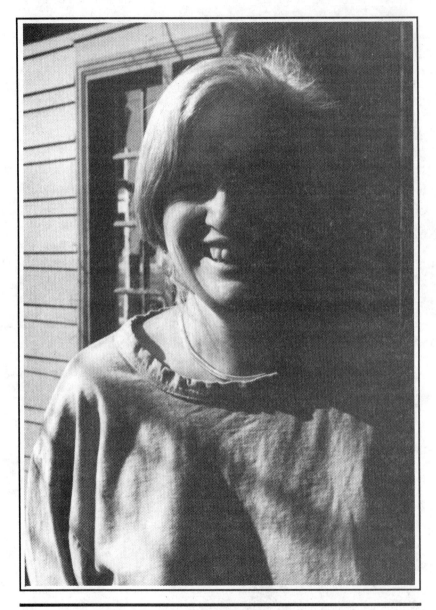

"Every part of life wants to be celebrated. Even the dark sides, the parts that are very painful."

6

Celebrating All Of Life
Susan Griffin

Perhaps because the bioregional movement originated largely among the more rugged, rural, back-to-the- landers, it has been relatively slow to appreciate the full importance of feminism. In recent years, however, the ecofeminism committee of the North American Bioregional Congress has been one of the most thoughtful and inspiring elements of the movement—a testimony of the truly revolutionary wisdom that feminism brings to bear upon our efforts to reconstruct society on a caring, nonviolent basis.

Susan Griffin is perhaps one of the most influential feminist writers of this age. Author of Woman & Nature: The Roaring Inside Her (Harper & Row, 1978), Pornography & Silence (Harper & Row, 1981) and several books of poetry, she lives in Berkeley, California. Her incisive yet poetic analysis of the culture of industrial society—the connections she makes between its treatment of nature and its treatment of women; its deeply militarist, racist and sexist fabric which enables it to isolate and then degrade other human beings and nature itself as "other"—stands as classic in its own time. Her own activist roots are deep in the fertile ground of the anti-war and anti-nuclear movements. Here, she speaks about the nature of the culture that has brought us to the brink, and the urgent need for alliances among the feminist, peace and ecology movements.

The New Catalyst: *What can you say about our culture's treatment of nature and the military character of our society?*

Susan Griffin: Well, they're very obviously connected, in terms of effects. For instance, the environment is now toxic with radiation waste, and radiation waste works synergistically with other kinds of pollution. It exacerbates the effects of the damage from pollution. So that just the problem of radiation waste alone, and contamination from sites all over the world, is very serious ecologically.

But there's also a whole different way to understand that connection which is psychologically and philosophically. In much of my work in *Woman and Nature* and *Pornography and Silence,* I looked at the way that this culture has a very problematic and alienated relationship with nature in which we basically posit the illusion that we can control nature. And we do that in two ways: one is through actually, directly, controlling nature; and the other is through the creation of the category of "otherness." (I'm taking that language from Simone de Beauvoir who first began to speak that way, referring to the female as the second sex.) And I think that's the paradigm category.

Then other categories follow suit, such as racism, and the creation of an enemy in a warfare mentality. Nuclear weapons have all been created in the context of the Cold War, in which we have an enemy, and the enemy is communism, the Soviet Union—the other guy who has a whole different approach to life. In the categorization of the other, what goes on is that we imagine ourselves in some way to be separate from nature and above nature. This shows in the religious idea that somehow the spirit is in distinction to the flesh; and the flesh belongs to the Devil, and the spirit to God. Through the theology of this particular civilization, women got identified with flesh and the devil. That was Eve's role in the Fall. And that identification is very deeply embedded in all our iconography and all our mythology and all our thinking, really. It's there as a sub- strata that has nothing to do with women, including thought about war.

In addition to that, the same qualities that we ascribe to women we also project pretty much on the enemy, whoever the enemy is, or on the category of the other—black people, Jews—depending who the focus is on. For instance, in the theological thinking of the middle ages, the interpretation of Eve's Fall was that she brought death into the world. If you think about that, if you're going to be projecting nature on to the other, then, of course, that other does bring death into the world. Because it's nature that has mortality, that has movement, that has life-cycles embedded into it. And it's that cyclical, natural process over which we do not have control that this culture has tried to remain in control of and tried to dominate. So that if you can dominate a woman, you can in a sense believe that you're not going to die.

I think the same thing is going on in this case with the Soviet Union—it could be anyone, picked out as an enemy. We look at them, and the arms race, for instance, as death. And if we can have more arms than they do, we have vanquished death. But that just doesn't hold any more. Quantity ceases to matter with nuclear weapons: that's not what it's about. And the Pentagon fully knows that. But they're also in a psychological sort of warfare. They're literally holding on to some belief or illusion that if they have more of these magical weapons, then they're going to keep death away. It's very primal sort of thought.

"In general, people who are more severely ill with dominance disease get power... and American society is very ill with dominance disease right now!"

TNC: *Your work brings together so much detail about the depradations of this civilization that I almost lose hope. It's so monolithic that I wonder how we get out of it?*

Susan Griffin: It's true that it's monolithic. But if you look at it like an illness that this culture is under the shadow of—with various degrees of severity—and someone who has it to a severe degree, sometimes expresses it as being a severe racist or a Nazi. But another thing that's available to them is to be a rapist or a pornographer. They're basically all expressions of the same illness. What's happening with someone who is severely ill with that—for whatever reasons—is that they have this system provided by the culture that is supposedly airtight which makes them feel that they have power over nature, power over life, over existence. Then what happens is that they take in a breath, or they feel sleepy, or they have a sexual feeling they didn't think they would have at a given moment, or they get hungry—their own body is nature, doing something to them, shaking them up. So they respond by getting more dominating, more aggressive. This is something I explained in *Pornography and Silence*: that far from pornography being a catharsis for those people who have a tendency in this direction, it can actually push them towards violence, because it's lending strength to that desire and telling them they can have power. But then every time they start to believe that, their own body proves them wrong. So they have to up the ante, and they get hooked, they get addicted.

TNC: *Would you say the same about militarism?*

Susan Griffin: Yes, exactly. So that war toys have to increase in the same way. Because it's an addiction. The real fear is of death. The real fear is of life. It's very telling that we have an economy in which the public roads are going to pot, the schools are crumbling away, we're demanding more and more proficiency and knowledge of people, but we're not bothering to educate our young people. And we're putting all this money into arms. We have serious domestic things to deal with and it all goes down the drain into war-toys.

For some reason—probably because it is a society of dominance—it makes sense that, in general, people who are more severely ill with dominance disease get power. That's not always true, but it's very true right now and American society is very ill with dominance disease right now!

But it's also true that there are a lot of people who are not in power who are thinking differently or who are just not so severely paralysed by this alienation—that's the case for most people—who see that the body *is* nature. And nature is not without meaning: this is what we're finally having to comprehend. And this paradigm that we've imposed over our own experience—that nature and culture, or matter and spirit, are separate—is not true. And that's what high energy physics has now understood: that matter and energy are on a continuum, energy being the modern inheritor of the concept of spirit. And the body continually reasserts itself, it won't let us lie. That's how powerful this wisdom is that's in our very selves, in our atoms, our very being.

"We lack strength because our roots are in the Earth, and our roots are also in community and in our connectedness with each other. And we've cut ourselves off from that."

TNC: *If that's true, then the question becomes: how do we create the conditions to enable that to emerge, as opposed to the culture of dominance?*

Susan Griffin: Well, I think that a lot of people *are* doing that. It's a time when we need to really listen to each other right now: the ecology movement and the peace movement *must* start listening to feminists. For a long time I felt that feminists needed to begin to make coalitions with other causes. I think that feminists are really moving in that direction now. Not as women joining male organizations, but working *with*. There still need to be all-female organizations. Because unfortunately women are still very oppressed economically, socially and politically. And that's true on the Left as well as in the mainstream. For example, among my friends doing theoretical work on peace, there's much more financial support for what men are doing.

TNC: *Do you have a vision of a culture that might be at peace in a different way?*

Susan Griffin: I don't have a wholly-wrought utopian vision, no. But I have had some wonderful experiences that act as pointers for my life.

One is that I'm very fortunate to be part of a group of people who all knew each other somewhat—not terribly close—but a sort of larger network of people. A friend of ours was killed quite suddenly almost three years ago now and, through the experience of her death and that grief, we got to know each other much more intimately. Because this friend—a peace activist—was very deeply committed to that work, and because the people who knew her and loved her share that same value system, we're becoming a genuine community. It's making me very aware of what a great need people have for that.

This rapacious picture of human nature that came about at the end of the 19th century with, first, Darwinism and then Social Darwinism is really inaccurate. Not only does it make rapaciousness and competitiveness and selfishness a virtue, it ignores other very real needs that people have. I think people really have the need to be in each others' lives. The biosphere is interdependent; and, like a forest, you can't study a tree without studying everything in that forest. And I think that's true of people, too. Of course, it's understood we're social animals. But there's some way in which we've never really done much about that, never really understood the need to have it existing in the actual structure of one's life.

TNC: *On a daily basis.*

Susan Griffin: Yes, on a daily basis.

The other day we were talking about the attraction of these fundamentalist, religious rights meetings, or New Agey spiritual get-togethers. People get very high off them and they feel this sense of connection with each other. But it isn't real. It doesn't last. It's like cotton candy. It's an illusory replacement for something we need, just like a drug addiction is.

You can also look at the military in that way, in that we in this culture really do lack strength. This obsession that we have with strength makes sense. We lack strength because our roots are in the Earth, and our roots are also in community and in our connectedness with each other. And we've cut ourselves off from all that. So we reach out to military weapons on the one hand and, on the other, to one-shot ecstatic experiences of communion with people. You're supposed to turn to your neighbour and say, "I love you," and you never see them after that!

I mean, after all, real love is not this romantic flash in the pan. It's something that's built over years. It's only recently that we've lived in these little tiny units, and they're not enough for people.

TNC: *Presumably there's a direct relationship between our atomization and our consequent respect and need for an authority figure, and—on the other side of that—the building of community and the taking of authority for our lives that* *we build together. Is that what you're saying?*

Susan Griffin: Absolutely. Yes. And I do think that there's something fundamental about size. I really agree with Schumacher, and I agree with a lot of anarchist work. We can think abstractly, but we don't think well out of context. Just like somebody who's drunk—this must be on my mind, I was out last night with someone who was drunk!—you know, someone who's drunk gets arrogant. They think they have these super-human abilities. You can get drunk on yourself out of context. Whereas, in context, we have much greater understandings. That's one of many reasons why, when a governmental unit gets too big, people's decisions become irrational. For instance, Berkeley is small enough that we have a feel for people who are sitting there up on the council. There's a real relationship there. You're not liable to make these people into either devils or super- humans, because there's some nitty-gritty going on.

"We have to begin to have faith in the life process... right now, in the midst of our protest, we have to begin practicing that."

TNC: *How do you work towards small-scale community at the same time as having to oppose society with mass action?*

Susan Griffin: There are two dangers I see for those of us who are America's dissidents. One is to blanketly distrust any use of media—like we're going to keep ourselves pure or something. We're going to go off and not be connected at all to what's happening. But you can't. There's no place you can go where the water's clean; there's no place you can go where the air's clean. It's not possible.

The other danger is to somehow become like the Democratic Party, for instance. The Democratic Party is like a co-alcoholic, with the Republican Party definitely being the alcoholic! Instead of thinking what are we about, and trying to bring it to fruition somehow, whether elected or not, the Democratic Party just forms itself into a pretzel shape in order to please. So you just lose your respect for them altogether—they'll do anything to get votes.

Let me use an analogy that I know very well. I teach writing, and I work with the creative process in a way that's similar to therapy but not therapy—it works with the emotional aspects of the writing process. One of the basic tenets of the way I work is to help my students enjoy their work. If you're forcing yourself, or doing it in a dutiful way, or you're bored, or you're not writing in the way you like but the way you think someone else wants, then it's going to be flat. It's not going to have the life-force in it.

TNC: *That's an analogy with politics?*

Susan Griffin: Right. I don't think the end justifies the means. Ever. Nature doesn't work that way. The means is always part of the end. What you're doing in the moment is all existence. There's no world except it exists at the moment. So if the means are horrible and you're doing that at the moment, that's what is. This idea that the means justify the end has got us into a terrible ecological mess. I think we need to keep that in mind as activists.

I got a letter from a wonderful woman called Fran Peavey who's an organizer and comedian. She was in India, and she was talking about one of her colleagues—an Indian man—who said to her, "You Americans always think in terms of the final effect of what you do—the goal. We in India don't think that way. If we believe in something, we'll do what we can, and we assume that it'll go into the field, and it'll affect things somehow. And the outcome may not be visible to us for quite a while. We may never know quite how it did it, but we have faith in this larger process."

I think we have to begin to have that faith in the life process. You see, the illness that we're suffering from in this culture is the lack of faith in life itself. So right now, in the midst of our very protest, we have to start practicing such faith.

Deena Metzger, who's a feminist and a wonderful poet, said (I wish I could quote her directly, because she said it beautifully, but I'm not good at memorizing words) something like, "The world is on fire. We're all in danger. There is only time to move slowly. There is only time to love."

TNC: *Is it true that, in the book you're currently working on, you're directing attention toward the nuclear dilemma?*

Susan Griffin: Yes. The whole book is an act of witnessing. I'm talking about the extraordinary qualities that come out in the people who have been able to survive Hiroshima, and the Holocaust. The act of witnessing is a beautiful part of life: the fact that matter desires consciousness and desires to witness and resonate and communicate. I want people to take that in, as much as the horror. Both. Because it's there. Every part of life wants to be celebrated. Even the dark sides, the parts that are very painful.

TNC: *Which takes us back to the beginning, that it's the fear of fear itself that is perhaps at the root of our civilization's problems. And that maybe respecting that fear, acknowledging it and living it, is a part of the solution?*

Susan Griffin: Yes, I really feel that is so.

"...we need people who, as a last resort, are willing to take things into their own hands and essentially become the forest in defence of itself: to go out and help big yellow machines find their true Dharma nature by returning to the Earth."

7

Becoming The Forest
In Defence Of Itself
Dave Foreman

Resisting the onslaught of the Megamachine, its unconscionable destruction of all in the path of profits, has united both city- and country-based bioregional activists in a common defence of nature. But the continuing worldwide destruction of forests and wildlife habitat has led to considerable debate within the environmental movement as to what strategy might best combat this abuse.

Dave Foreman, one of the founders of the "radical environmentalist" group, Earth First! and author of Ecodefense: A Field Guide To Monkey-Wrenching (Ned Ludd Books, 1987), has argued for many years in favor of tree-spiking and monkey-wrenching as being among the most succesful ways of preventing further destruction of the Earth's wild lands. Fully aware that the Empire was striking back, as he puts it, it is ironic that, just months after this interview, he and several other Earth First! activists were arrested in a major infiltration operation by the FBI clearly designed to neutralize what had become an overly effective organization. Foreman's comments are consequently of abiding interest in the search for appropriate strategies of continued resistance.

The New Catalyst: *You have a reputation for being an environmental evangelist. Where does this reputation come from, and what leads you to write a book like* Ecodefense?

Dave Foreman: Part of the reason is because my speaking style comes from the same origins as Jimmy Swaggart or Martin Luther King—the southern evangelism which I was brought up in.

Also I think it's because *Earth First!* has represented a sort of fundamentalist revival within the environmental movement—a return to the basics of John Muir and Aldo Leopold, people like that—getting back to the roots of an ethical commitment. We *do* talk about ethics, about values. We've also used quite a bit of music in our work which I think ties in with it.

But as to where I'm coming from, I'm basically a conservative person. What led me to *Ecodefense* was trying, through all the steps of the process, to preserve wilderness and natural diversity, and being frustrated seeing that the system really isn't legitimate, it works on the basis of co-option and compromise. I finally came to the realization that in order to save natural diversity and see evolution continue, we have to question the fundamental basis of western civilization.

TNC: *Who were you working with before* Earth First!*?*

Dave Foreman: I worked for the Wilderness Society for eight years during the 1970s as their south west representative, and then as their chief lobbyist in Washington, D.C.

TNC: *And that wasn't achieving anything?*

Dave Foreman: It was basically achieving crumbs. We were getting wilderness areas, yes, but they were rocks and ice. They weren't biologically productive old-growth forests; they weren't grizzly bear habitat. It seemed that we were preserving a scenic system of outdoor gymnasiums. What we wanted to do with *Earth First!* was get the discussion back to its basics: that we're talking about natural diversity; about three and a half billion years of evolution—the continuation of evolution.

"We aren't talking about scenery or some back-packing parks for urban yuppies. We're talking about *life*, and what kind of future is going to exit."

TNC: *Do you have statistics as to how bad the crisis is, in terms of wilderness and wildlife?*

Dave Foreman: I can't imagine any grimmer statistics than the ones Michael Soulé, David Ehrenfeld and other conservation biologists put out. For example, one third of all species on the planet may become extinct in the next 20 years. By the end of the century, the only large mammals left will be those we *choose* to allow to exist. Michael Soulé is saying that, because of human activity, vertebrate evolution is esentially at an end. That's just astounding! And those aren't comments from a bunch of radical environmentalists who don't know anything. They are from the most prominent ecologists and field ecologists in the world.

All we have to do is look at the systemic effects we're having on the whole life-support system of the planet. The destruction of the ozone layer, the greenhouse effect, changes in weather patterns, the fact that penguin blubber in the Antarctic is loaded with DDT and radiation.... We have become a force of change on this planet that exceeds even geological forces. Right now we are seeing the highest rate of extinction ever known in three and a half billion years of evolution; higher than 65 million years ago at the end of the Cretaceous and the extinction of the dinosaurs.

So we aren't talking about saving scenery or some back- packing parks for urban yuppies. We're talking about *life*, and what kind of future is going to exist. Is the characteristic megafauna a thousand years from now going to be rats and cockroaches? Or are there still going to be some great blue whales and redwoods and grizzly bears?

TNC: *There are many groups and communities in British Columbia who are having to organize against logging—our number one problem. How would you suggest people do that?*

Dave Foreman: I'm a real believer in diversity. If diversity is good for an ecosystem, it's good for a social movement as well. We need the whole range of approaches from people studying old growth forests, to people researching the economics of it, showing that most logging is welfare logging, that it really doesn't pay for itself. We need people trying to come up with alternative approaches for utilization of wood fibre: how do we live with a lighter impact on the planet? We need people trying to do basic education to the public, trying to create a better social and political atmosphere in which these decisions can be made. We need people lobbying. We need people filing law suits.

But we also need people engaging in nonviolent civil disobedience. And we need people who, as a last resort, are willing to take things into their own hands and essentially become the forest in defence of itself: to go out and help big yellow machines find their true Dharma nature by returning to the Earth. And by innoculating trees with metal spikes.

"I'm a real believer in diversity. If diversity is good for an ecosystem, it's good for a social movement as well."

TNC: *How would you expand on that difference, strategically speaking, between civil disobedience and direct action of the monkey-wrenching variety?*

Dave Foreman: Civil disobedience has come out of a largely Christian tradition that's interested in the means as much as the ends. For many

Christian peace activists, or civil rights activists who engage in civil disobedience, witnessing for peace—standing up for what is good—is as important as the results. For those people, being arrested, going to jail, suffering, is part of it; it's partly a personal transformation that they're after.

My major concern, though, is seeing big trees, and untouched watersheds, and wildlife habitat remain. So I'm more interested in results. And I think with monkey-wrenching, a person doesn't care about taking credit for it, about their personal growth, about racking up brownie points in heaven because of their suffering or whatever. They want to save trees. And, of course, then you have to be very careful that you don't get into an attitude where the ends justify the means. You have to be constantly thoughtful about what you're doing, and be very careful with it.

TNC: *Not become a hero?*

Dave Foreman: Right. Another real problem with monkey-wrenching, and one that we very much need to work on, is that in our society we've forgotten how to be ethical warriors. How to be warriors on one level, and take a confrontational, No Compromise attitude towards the forest service, say—which is what we need to do—but then to step back within our groups and communities and develop a compromising, listening, problem-solving, mutually respectful relationship with other people when you have questions or disagreements. Too often we take this No Compromise, us-versus-them attitude back into our own councils and we fight the same way with each other as we do, say, with the forest service. I think the whole tenor of the recent deep ecology/social ecology debate has been a wonderful example of that.

In hunter-gatherer tribes, there were rituals and other types of cleansing ceremonies, both to prepare oneself for potential violence and then to de-program and get back into the community after it was over. We don't have that today in our society. That's certainly one of the things that the bioregional movement could work on.   Another aspect of this is that we like to pretend that all the problems of the world are the result of a few wealthy white males who run corporations. That it's all on their shoulders. I think that's a cop-out because all of us in our lifestyles and our involvement with modern society are partly responsible for the destruction going on. It's the old Pogo cartoon: that we've met the enemy and it is us! We all have to take responsibility and recognize that we're all partly to blame. We can all begin to move as well as we can individually in the direction of causing less damage, and of having more of a steady state, non-impacting role.

TNC: *You've mentioned in your introduction to the second edition of*

Ecodefense *that the Empire is striking back. When it actually comes down to doing some monkey-wrenching, people are afraid of being caught. How can we deal with this fear? How can we move towards a more offensive position?*

Dave Foreman: I think the Empire *is* striking back even more than when I wrote that introduction. For example in the United States now, tree-spiking is a federal felony. It was included in the comprehensive drug bill last fall. And the Forest Service is turning all their marijuana cops loose on monkey-wrenchers as well. There are $25,000 rewards out in various states now for monkey-wrenchers. But as the other side improves its techniques, we're also improving our techniques. For example, the supplement to the second edition of *Ecodefense* will have a section on how to guard against informants, or infiltrators, and *agent-provocateurs.*

But the simple fact remains that very very few monkey- wrenchers have been caught. The only ones who have been caught that I know of have been caught because of their own carelessness. You owe it to yourself not to be caught. If you live in a small community, you may be better off not monkey-wrenching nearby, but going somewhere else— maybe having a work exchange agreement where somebody 500 miles away comes and monkey-wrenches in your area, and you do it in her area.... Or you may not want to get involved publicly as a wilderness supporter in an area you plan to monkey-wrench. In most cases, if you think before you act, it's very very difficult for anybody to be caught.

For example, the National Forest system in the United States has 375,000 miles of road. They can't guard all of those roads. A million acres a year of the National Forests is being logged. They can't guard that whole million acres....

TNC: *Blockading and civil defence have ended up with people paying stiff fines and even going to jail, and it doesn't do much to save the trees. How effective is monkey-wrenching?*

Dave Foreman: There are two levels on which we have to try to gauge its effectiveness. One is the very site specific level: you go in, you spike some trees, you destroy bulldozers, whatever: do you save that place? And I think there's a mixed bag of success there. I know of certain timber stands in the Pacific Northwest that have been spiked that are still standing after several years. And in other cases that got a high public profile, the Forest Service or whoever have gone in to save face and have spent more money to extract spikes from the trees than the trees were worth. So there's a trade-off as to whether you really want publicity or not, because you may force your opponent into a face-saving posture.

But the other level on which to gauge monkey-wrenching is a larger level that we haven't achieved yet, but which is the basic strategy behind it: that if you have thousands of people out taking care of big yellow machines on controversial timber sales, on a North American scale, or a world scale, before long the insurance companies that insure those machines will not insure them any more, or the premiums will go up so much that no company can afford to pay them. That means that it will become economically even less profitable to go into these virgin areas. And fairly large tracts of generally wild country would revert back to an unmanaged condition. We haven't achieved that level of monkey-wrenching yet where we can see if that is effective, but that is the goal. There are 12,000 copies of *Ecodefense* out now in peoples' hands all over the world.

"Is there room in our world view for other mammals, for birds, for large ecosystems that are not manipulated by human beings? That's what it all boils down to."

TNC: *Some people would argue that monkey-wrenching is a violent act. How would you respond to that?*

Dave Foreman: It depends on how you define violence. For example, it's called "terrorism" and to me, if pulling up survey stakes is terrorism but bombing civilians from 30,000 feet in a B-52 is "peace-keeping," then words have no meaning. It's doublespeak. I don't think monkey-wrenching is violence if you define violence as something against other life-forms. And I'm not sure that violence in and of itself is evil. Any creature will defend itself violently if pushed into a corner, and I don't think that we overcome our problems by denying that basic animal instinct of self-preservation.

TNC: *What about the argument that it's an offence against someone's private property to monkey-wrench a bulldozer?*

Dave Foreman: I think the whole concept of private property as an ultimate "good" has got to be replaced. There's a higher good out there than private property. A bulldozer is inherently a destructive agent. It can be used for good under certain circumstances, but its primary function is destruction. If they keep their bulldozers away from wild country, I'm not going to touch them. But when their bulldozer invades a wild place that I'm defending, then it's just self-defence. It's very easy not to have your machinery destroyed: just stay away from wild places!

TNC: *Another argument against tree-spiking is that the workers in the forest can get hurt. Is that proven?*

Dave Foreman: Well, I think we've got to look at just how dangerous logging is. Last year in Washington, I believe, there were some 30 people killed in logging accidents. It's the most dangerous occupation in North America. So far there's only been one person injured by tree-spiking—the incident at Louisiana Pacific mill in California—and that was such a bizarre, unusual case that it's really not a good example. It was not done by *Earth First!* or for ecological reasons at all.

The purpose of tree-spiking is to keep trees from being cut down. If the tree is cut down, then you've failed. And so you have to give some kind of warning, by spray-painting the tree, or sending some kind of safe communiqué. If a company knows that the trees are spiked and chooses to send a crew in to cut them down, then there's the question: whose responsibility is it, if somebody gets hurt? And if a worker chooses to go ahead, knowing they've been spiked, then whose responsibility is it?

TNC: *In terms of the global crisis, what do you think are the most serious issues and how do we even get close to dealing with them?*

Dave Foreman: I really think there's only one issue and that's the question of natural diversity. Everything else, in one way or another, ties into that question. Right now we have one species, *homo sapiens*, that's taking 30 per cent of the total photosynthetic energy output of the planet for its use. That's extraordinary when you realize that there are several million species on the planet. And so the question is the carrying capacity of the Earth versus the number and the impact of human beings, and what is our proper role? Where is the balance? Is there room in our world view for other mammals, for birds, for large ecosystems that are not manipulated by human beings? That's what it all boils down to.

The question of natural diversity applies also to social issues. We are seeing human beings around the world—all five and a half billion of us—hammered into one global society where cultural differences are losing their importance as we become this one business culture. The multinational corporations have become more important than tribes or nations. We need to respect the cultural diversity of the planet. And oftentimes that's one of the things that is destroyed along with natural diversity.

The next several decades are going to be the most tumultuous time on Earth for human beings. We are not immune from biology. If you look at human beings, we are in the classic J-shaped curve: our population growth, our development of technology, our production of toxins—it's all on an exponential curve. In biology, the only way those curves end is by a sudden drop. And in many cases, the larger the population, the more likely it is that they become extinct.

TNC: *Lots of people feel powerless about this. What can people do?*

Dave Foreman: A lot of would-be activists are so frustrated with the enormity of the problem and not knowing where to start, that they never begin at all. We've got to get out of that way of thinking and realize that if we can save one tree, if we can save one acre of grizzly bear habitat, one wolf, then we've done something. Each little step like that is part of the solution to the larger problem. When you start doing something— particularly something so individually empowering as monkey-wrenching—you say, "I don't have to convince anybody. I don't have to manipulate the system. I don't have to go and debate with anyone. I can just go out and *do* this myself, take the responsibility for it, connect on a one-to-one basis with the wilderness." That is incredibly empowering and extremely healthy.

"If we can save one tree, if we can save one acre of grizzly bear habitat, one wolf, then we've done something. Each little step like that is part of the solution to the larger problem."

So there are two things to do right now. One is this self-defence of the wild. More of us need to do everything we can to try to ensure that wild places remain, and that's whether you monkey-wrench, or just buy wild land, or whether you work through the political process for better management, whatever.

The other is what the bioregional movement is doing: trying to re-connect with our tribal roots, trying to recreate, to grope towards, that kind of society. And none of us are going to achieve that. It's going to be generations from now because we're so far removed from the natural world. But at least we're laying the groundwork. I see ecodefense and bioregionalism as being the two sides of the path towards whatever society will become in the future, once we're through this catastrophic event that's coming up.

(The Earth First! Journal *can be contacted c/- P.O. Box 7, Canton, NY 13617, U.S.A.*)

"The deep ecologists see that there is something fundamentally wrong with our philosophy, with our spiritual life, with our values, and with our whole society, and that mere reforms may be worse than doing nothing at all because they give people a sense that something is happening when, in fact, nothing *is* happening."

8

Deep Ecology Down Under
John Seed

Deep ecology is a significant strand of the bioregional philosophy. So termed by Norwegian philosopher, Arne Naess, to distinguish it from what he calls "shallow environmentalism" which works for minor reforms to the industrial system, deep ecologists seek major changes in the way those of us in dominant society view, and act in, the world. A primary shift required by the perspective of deep ecology is to a biocentric way of being: seeing all of life as sacred, not merely human beings, and acting upon that belief in all of our decisions.

John Seed was a back-to-the-lander, living simply and growing avocadoes in New South Wales, Australia, until Earth-raping machinery arrived on his doorstep. The ensuing struggle to save the forest in his immediate vicinity quickly propelled him into full-time activism in defence of the world's rain-forests, and into becoming an active proponent of deep ecology. Co-author with Joanna Macy, Pat Fleming and Arne Naess of Thinking Like A Mountain: Towards A Council Of All Beings *(New Society Publishers, 1988), John Seed has toured Europe and Turtle Island for Earth First! on more than one occasion. His discussion of Australia's alternative scene reveals the similarities with that of Turtle Island, and just how far and wide bioregional ideas are spread.*

The New Catalyst: *Can you tell us more about the destruction of the tropical rainforests, especially in Australia?*

John Seed: In Australia we've been struggling to protect the rain-forests since 1979. The rainforests in Australia stretch right along the east coast, from the southern most temperate rainforests in Tasmania to the more tropical rainforests in Queensland about 3,000 miles to the north. They're just in tiny little patches and if you put them all together, in a circle, they'd have a radius of only about 70 kilometres—about one thousandth of Australia's land area; but it contains about one-third of all our species of plants and animals. This is pretty typical of rainforests around the world which is why they have been called the womb of life because, world-wide, they contain about half of the world's ten million species of plants and animals.

TNC: *What is happening to the Australian rainforests?*

John Seed: In New South Wales and Tasmania, where our first two campaigns took place, there have been certain successes in protecting them. But, in Queensland, where the majority of the rainforests and the genetically most valuable tropical rainforests are situated, the position is very, very poor, and very few of them are protected. Even where they are protected in National Parks it's a very temporary designation. Parliament can easily revoke designations for some other purpose, and it commonly does. The main campaign in Australia is to protect Queensland's tropical rainforest where there's logging, about 3,000 small tin mines, there's real estate, and a very destructive "Miami Beach" kind of tourism.

"Satellite photographs show that the rainforests are disappearing at quite an incredible rate: a football field a second is one way of trying to grasp it, or an area the size of Switzerland every year."

TNC: *Do you have any idea of how quickly they are being depleted?*

John Seed: It's very much as it is world-wide. Probably less than a single human generation remains before they're either annihilated or reduced to such a small size that they can no longer maintain their species composition and the genetic diversity that is necessary. Rainforests require a tremendous area in one patch because of the huge number of species—they start to simplify as soon as you bring them down below a certain size.

TNC: *What effect would that have in Australia specifically?*

John Seed: It would mean that a large proportion of Australia's plant and animal species would become extinct. This is happening. It would be catastrophic as far the biological nature of Australia is concerned.

TNC: *What about the world-wide situation?*

John Seed: Satellite photographs show that the rainforests are disappearing at quite an incredible rate: a football field a second is one way of trying to grasp it, or an area the size of Switzerland every year. There's no sign of this abating. This indicates that the world's rainforests will be destroyed within a lifetime. In India, for example, less than five years remain before the Kipling jungles—there are four patches left—will all have fallen below the minimum critical size necessary for their continued survival and evolution. In the Solomon Islands, seven or eight years remain. I'd say half of the rainforest countries in the world will have totally destroyed their rainforests by the turn of the century at present rates. The pressure is now on the states of Sarawak in Borneo and Sabat. We've got a strong campaign along with the Penan who are the last of the nomadic hunter/gatherer cultures that are still viable in southeast Asia—we're actually doing a blockade right at the moment to try and stop the logging on their land.

TNC: *We're more familiar with the Central American situation—Brazil in particular—where the Amazon is being destroyed for hamburgers. What can you tell us about that?*

John Seed: In Central America especially, probably half the rainforests have now been destroyed, mainly for cheap pasture for growing cattle and mainly for the cheap end of the American market. It's said that this results in the drop of about a dime in the price of a hamburger in America. One of the companies that has actually admitted to using this rainforest beef is Burger King. So there's been a strong campaign, especially by the Earth First! organization, to boycott Burger King. In fact, May of 1987 was Whopper Stopper month in America [a campaign directed against Burger King and others' despoliation of the rainforest], and Burger King sales dropped 12 per cent.

The other big campaign at the moment is to stop the World Bank and the other multi-lateral development banks from funding these sorts of developments. The World Bank is probably the single largest force in the destruction of the rainforests in the world today. For instance, the Narmada Valley scheme, in India: the World Bank has a multi-billion dollar scheme to put in 3,000 dams. This will result in the destruction of most of the forests there and the displacement of tribal peoples. Influencing the lending policy of the World Bank and the other multi-lateral development banks is probably the most important thing one can do. While we can't influence countries like India very easily, let alone Brazil and Indonesia, we *can* influence the World Bank whose decisions are made in proportion to the amount of money a country lends. On September 30, 1986 there was a day of protest at their meeting in Washington, where the Rainforest Action Network unfurled a big banner, and in Canberra, in Denmark and Holland and Japan—I think eight or ten countries participated.

TNC: *What other direct actions have been taken in Australia?*

John Seed: In 1979 the first direct actions took place in Terranea Creek. That's how I first became involved. I was living about five miles from there, up in the hills: back to the land, growing macadamia nuts and avocadoes and mangoes and so on. But 1979 intruded into paradise! At that time, hundreds of people were arrested. We put ourselves between the machines and the wilderness.

"It's all theatre of social change, where you've got to do something either violent or clever, in order to get on the agenda, to get into the papers, to attract peoples' attention."

TNC: *Can you describe what you were doing?*

John Seed: At Terranea Creek, we climbed up trees, walked in front of the bulldozers, people chained themselves to machinery, and so on. The next big campaign was in Tasmania to stop the damming of the Franklin River which was going to flood the temperate rainforest wilderness. There we had blockades with yellow inflatable rafts and all manner of things.

In 1983 and 1984, in the tropical rainforests of Queensland, people took direct action by climbing high up in trees. We also found a place which was the only possible route through which the machines could pass to build a road through the heart of the national park. We dug holes in the road at that point and cast cement blocks in the bottom of the holes, with steel reinforcing in the cement and with high tensile chain coming out of the reinforcing. We had fifty dollar padlocks on the end of the chain so that when the machinery came, people jumped into these holes and padlocked their ankles to the cement pads at the bottom, and then we filled the holes back up again so that all that was visible to the drivers were these heads sticking out of the ground! The drivers had the choice of calling the police to dig people out, or crushing the people. We held them up for days and days there while they dug people out, and we got a lot of publicity—it was very photogenic. It's all theatre of social change, where you've got to do something either violent or clever, in order to get on the agenda, to get into the papers, to attract peoples' attention.

TNC: *How do you feel about the destruction of property?*

John Seed: There hasn't been much of that in Australia. I've got no objections to it myself, but I'm not interested in doing anything that's going to alienate the protection of nature from a wide community of people. Because even if, in the end, you can save something by sabotaging it, by making the trees worthless and so on, it's really the planet or nothing now. That means there's got to be a deep sweeping change throughout human beings, and all of the things we do have to be aimed and directed towards that. There's really not that much point in saving this piece of ground, or that forest, because it's all going to disappear within a generation or two regardless of any temporary victories we may have *unless* there's really a profound change in human beings.

TNC: *That raises the question of values and deep ecology. Does deep ecology have much of a following in Australia?*

John Seed: Yes, many have heard of it. The term was coined ten years ago by Arne Naess who's the emeritus professor of philosophy at Oslo University, a renowned Spinoza scholar, and also a lover of wild nature who has taken environmental action over the years. He made this distinction between the deep, long-range ecology movement and what he called reformist environmentalism—those people who think that small adjustments are all that is needed in order to protect nature. The deep ecologists see that there is something fundamentally wrong with our philosophy, with our spiritual life, with our values, and with our whole society, and that mere reforms may be worse than doing nothing at all because they give people a sense that something is happening when, in fact, nothing *is* happening. So, deep ecology is looking for a total reconceptualization and reidentification so that we come to see that we are indeed part of nature, that this isn't just poetic. Any attempt to fulfill ourselves at the expense of nature is misguided. Even when people have intellectually rejected this idea, it nonetheless permeates the very air that we breathe and the values of our culture.

The truth is that if we destroy the Earth, we destroy ourselves. When we destroy the millions of species in the rainforests, then we're basically unravelling the fabric of life out of which all our economics and politics and religion and everything else grows. Once people come to this basic realization then there's no longer the tendency to get into games of compromise. It's a much deeper problem.

TNC: *What's the situation with respect to uranium mining in Australia?*

John Seed: We're pretty disappointed because, in the last elections, the Labour Party promised that they would close down the uranium mines and industry in Australia. But after their election, they opened Roxby Downs which some say is going to be the biggest uranium mine in the world. Australians are lazy—everyone is just too interested in getting a new car. That sort of spirit of materialism has really defeated the opposition for the time being. There have been lots of actions against uranium mining, hundreds of people have been arrested at Roxby Downs trying to stop it, but I don't think there's been much success.

TNC: *In our struggles to deal with the logging issue here in British Columbia, many environmental groups have been able to form really useful alliances with the native people who are also struggling for their land. Are there similar alliances in Australia?*

John Seed: From time to time. But I don't think you could say it's similar at the moment. Aboriginals as a group are not necessarily the beautiful ecologists that people often project on to them. In fact, some of the land councils in the northern territory are pro-uranium mining because of the royalties that they will receive.

"When we destroy the millions of species in the rainforests, then we're basically unravelling the fabric of life out of which all our economics and politics and religion and everything else grows."

TNC: *What about the back-to-the-land movement: is that very much a part of the alternative?*

John Seed: Yes, it is. There was a big wave in the early '70s which resulted in tens of thousands of people resettling certain areas, creating a very strong alternative society. Exactly how strong the alternative is now remains to be seen. People tend to slip back pretty easily into their old ways and, after a while, what was going to be their simple house doesn't seem to be enough. There's solar electricity, and then there's this and that, and it becomes more like a different costume than any really fundamental change—which is what we believed it was going to be. There are a lot of people who just sort of look the part, and it's pretty hard to distinguish them from the generally- hedonistic, Me-first society out there.

TNC: *How do you see us getting away from the Me- first mentality?*

John Seed: Probably through a deepening of the sense of who *I* actually am. When I realize that I don't have any independent existence, that I am part of a food chain, for instance, then at a certain point Me-first and Earth- first become inseparable. I feel that's the best position to be coming from—to realize one's identity with the Earth. "Myself" now includes the rainforest, it includes clean air and water.

I sometimes think wryly that the story of the ten commandments—the old testament, the new testament—it's all bullshit, really. It's just been golden calf since time immemorial and nothing ever really changed. The Jews thought they'd changed it, so did the Christians. It's just this most incredible and fervent religion the world's ever known, this worship of *stuff*, of *things*, of *objects*—idolatry. Well, we can't really afford five billion materialists: there just isn't enough material to support them!

TNC: *Does this concern for the ecology of the planet, and the desire for a spiritual connection to that, translate in Australia into Green politics?*

John Seed: There's one political party—the Australian Democrats—that has a pretty good environmental platform, and there have been various attempts to start Green Parties. But there's nothing really gelled together the way that it has in Europe. Yet there's a growing movement of people looking around for a model that does fit with reality. We get together on the solstices and equinoxes and hold rituals to bond with the Earth and to get rid of the sense of alienation and separation.

(The Rainforest Information Centre can be contacted at: P.O. Box 368, Lismore, N.S.W. 2480, Australia; in North America, contact the Rainforest Action Network, 300 Broadway, Suite 28, San Francisco, CA 94133, USA.)

*

"A North American Indian philosopher has likened the relationship between women and men to the eagle, which soars to unbelievable heights and has tremendous power on two equal wings—one female, one male—carrying the body of life between them."

*

9

Wings Of The Eagle

Marie Wilson

O ne of the avowed aims of bioregionalists is to work to become "native to place" as human groups once were, before the advent of industrial civilization. Accordingly, bioregionalists have a natural affinity with indigenous peoples, deeply respecting the fact of their survival through the ages, and seeing their ways as something of a model for a sustainable future. Descriptive of this affinity is Akwesasne Notes' term for both as "Native and Natural peoples." Support for native groups in their contemporary struggles to survive and to assert their autonomy has been at the heart of much bioregional work.

Marie Wilson is a spokesperson for the Gitksan Wet'suwet'en Tribal Council from north western British Columbia. The Gitksan Wet'suwet'en have been involved, since 1987, in a classic native land claims case against both the provincial and federal governments. Seeking to assert their claim to over 22,000 square miles of their traditional territory, the tribal council took their case to the British Columbia Supreme Court. There they have had to defend themselves against charges that the Gitksan Wet'suwet'en were no longer a distinct culture, since they were assimilated into the dominant society by virtue of their living in modern houses and purchasing "white" consumer goods. As a cultural reseacher for the tribal council, Marie Wilson has been involved in gathering evidence to demonstrate that, despite this attempt to deny their existence as an authentic culture, her people are indeed distinct and have never ceded their lands to the Canadian state.

While the case drags on slowly through the courts—deliberately prolonged by governments that fear the effect of its resolution in favor of the Gitksan Wet'suwet'en—resource extraction has continued apace in the territory under dispute. Subsequently, in 1989, the native people took to blockading logging roads in their home region in order to prevent further destruction of the forests.

Widely supported by environmentalists and other non-Indians, the tribal council envisages a partnership model of bioregional government, involving both Indians and non-Indians, should the case be resolved in its favor. Yet many non-native people remain fearful of what Indian self-government might mean. In this interview, Marie Wilson talks about some of the differences in outlook of the two cultures, pointing to ways in which we might come to a closer understanding of one another.

The New Catalyst: *Many non-native activists believe we have much to learn from native peoples. I'd like to explore some of the similarities and differences that exist between native and non-native cultures, so we might better understand one another.*

For example, the ideas of ecofeminism suggest that the ways in which women have been mistreated by patriarchal society are very similar to the ways in which nature has been ravished and exploited. What do you think?

Marie Wilson: When I read about ecofeminism I find that the attitudes towards women and the feelings inside myself are different. It's difficult to explain, but it's as if women are separate. Though I agree with the analysis, the differences must be because of where I come from. In my mind, when I speak about women, I speak about humanity because there is equality in the Gitksan belief: the human is one species broken into two necessary parts, and they are equal. One is impotent without the other.

When I look upon the Western world today, I see this human species broken into a siamese twin relationship where one wounded partner is being dragged behind the other. There is no co-operation, or pragmatic understanding, which is necessary for the species to be whole.

A North American Indian philosopher has likened the relationship between women and men to the eagle, which soars to unbelievable heights and has tremendous power on two equal wings—one female, one male—carrying the body of life between them. The moment one is fractured or harmed in any way, then that powerful bird is doomed to remain on the earth and cannot reach those heights.

We tend to think: male, female—two species. We are not. We are one. Therefore I am feminine to the largest degree but I cannot bring myself to hurt or blame that male part of me that has come from my body: my sons. Similarly, my husband. It's a wonderful feeling to be loved, after 40 years, to have support and oneness with someone. It hasn't always been easy. As you can see, I'm not a submissive woman and he came from a rather chauvinistic family; we had a lot of growing up to do. Coming straight out of our Gitksan background, however, was a deep commitment to our union. Though Jeff has been a loving father, the children are my responsibility—by my example I will mark them.

TNC: *Perhaps in a culture that is connected to the land, and isn't separated from the life process, there is a greater appreciation and understanding of the Earth as Mother?*

Marie Wilson: I don't look upon the Earth as my mother. I don't believe the Gitksan ever did. They talked instead of the Power Larger Than Ourselves. They looked upon the land, the sea, the air, the creatures, as created life. Other native peoples did have a vision of the Earth as mother, but I can only speak for Gitksan.

The ground is throbbing with life, the dirt is not really dirt, in a sense, it is full of life. We are a product of the dust of the stars, as others have said. This hand that I hold up is actually a multitude of different organisms living off of the kernel that is my life. There are thousands of different, created things within my body that have nothing to do with the spark that causes our energy to flow. We are the compost of the future. This is exactly the vision that Gitksan have. What do we cherish most in the corner of our gardens? The compost. Where do we put it? Around the tender new life to give it a good start in the new created life it will become. If I had any way of describing myself, that would be the way I would like to be described. I believe this is why the Gitksan believed in reincarnation. They believed that the energy that I create cannot be destroyed—you can change its appearance but the influence remains.

"A North American Indian philosopher has likened the relationship between women and men to the eagle, which soars to unbelievable heights and has tremendous power on two equal wings—one female, one male—carrying the body of life between them."

The Gitksan did not have a god in the sky. They had a power larger than themselves which they recognized; they understood the limit of a lifespan and they lived comfortably within that limit. It was this understanding that was fundamental to the covenant created between humans and the land. They knew that the well-being of future generations depended upon caring for all life which the land itself represents. The land is the skin of the Earth— without it, we die. And yet, we're ripping the skin off the Earth without any thought at all, not appreciating that that first inch of soil represents life.

TNC: *The Gitksan's sense of spirituality would never have allowed the destruction of that inch?*

Marie Wilson: Oh no! We believe that each created life is so born as to survive, knowing its own way. If we leave it alone, it will survive. We understand that we must use what we must to survive—that in order for one life to survive, another must be given. The Gitksan had ways of cleansing themselves before entering the animal world to take life—actually to receive life, to accept the gift. The hunters cleansed themselves not for a good hunt but so they would be acceptable to the animal. This is a total difference in attitude.

The Gitksan have no word for sin. Instead, you make bad judgements. Bad judgements have to do with people and have nothing to do with a god. All actions come back, full circle, and we have a lot to account for.

So my relationship as a woman is often different from the vision that non-Indian women have in their heads about being a woman. My vision as a woman is not bitter, although I think women have suffered bitterly in the world. I believe that there's no way that any woman can cut herself off from that—we are sisters. My feeling for women involves almost a pity for humanity because we have missed the boat so badly. The Gitksan are not alone. There are so many cultures who believe the same thing we do.

"I believe all people started out connected to the land. People like the Gitksan copied nature because they were surrounded by it, not protected from it as we are. They saw the cycle of life, from the very smallest to the largest, all connected, and saw that the system itself punished any breaking of the cycle—not a god."

TNC: *Yes, people who were not brought up this way are looking towards cultures like the Gitksan for some direction.*

Marie Wilson: The pity is that I believe all people started out connected to the land. People like the Gitksan copied nature because they were surrounded by it, not protected from it as we are. They saw the cycle of life, from the very smallest to the largest, all connected, and saw that the system itself punished any breaking of the cycle—not a god. The people saw and understood the checks and balances that were exhibited by the cycle and chose to base their fundamental truths and authority and responsibilities on something that has worked for millions of years. They fitted themselves to the cycle of life.

What we are doing is putting into the English language what we have in our heads. This is very difficult to do. It can take months to define a few words: creation, philosophy, self-government, spirit.

TNC: *How is respect for other life made concrete in Gitksan society?*

Marie Wilson: It's made concrete through the rules. People have asked what is our law. We called them rules because we have no outside control; we used inner control. We didn't have judges or lawyers or supreme courts or anything like that. So the people had to know themselves in order to control themselves. Individuals were under strict self-control and, collectively, this controlled the whole society.

The principles, or rules, were about hunting, about relationships between humans. Self-cleansing before hunting included fasting and meditation, and the hunters removed themselves from the women so that they could go deeply into themselves. In the kill itself there were certain things that had to be done in order to honor that creature: ways of disposing of what was not used, for example, though almost everything was used. Most of what they did was based on common sense which included reason and flexibility, because no two situations are quite the same.

The criteria for judgement were that decisions must be good for the people, not just the decision-maker. While people of today dismiss this process as belonging to a primitive time when people were limited, does this mean that today peoples' lives are any less significant? And who will make the choice as to who is expendable and who is not? People in the so-called western world may be materially wealthy, but they are bankrupt in morals. The conditions under which people in less wealthy nations live—including the native peoples in this country—have meant that they are the recipients for decisions made by people who have set themselves up as gods.

You must realize that in my language there is no word for "rights." We have really struggled to find an equivalent in Gitksan-Wet'suwet'en and there is none. The closest we could come to an equivalent was jurisdiction and responsibility. We have obligation and control, and the responsibility that goes with it. "Rights," to us, is a very selfish word.

TNC: *Today, we may need more emphasis on responsibility: the other side of the rights coin. Women have clamored for rights—equal slices of a rotten pie—when we've had all the responsibility.*

Marie Wilson: I have the same attitude towards women who reach points of great authority and they feel they must equate that authority to male authority. That is totally wrong because the moment they start pretending that they are not female, they turn into almost skirted males! I resent that because the world needs the power of women in these positions of authority. I never forget for a moment that I am female even though I am a highly political person. Men must become capable of discussing a woman's position, not her body. We must never forget who we are as women.

TNC: *In fact, some of us have to remember. The world needs our voice. Do you feel it is possible to have caring, loving relations extended beyond the couple? Perhaps not with the same intensity but so that we are ready to take care of each other beyond just our families?*

Marie Wilson: We do have real affection for young people who are having similar struggles as we have had. We needn't even know them. Children in the Gitksan were loved and taught, not as a privilege or a right, but as an investment in the future comfort and continuation of the society.

TNC: *I was at a native feast not so long ago and all ages of people were there—from the very young to the very old. It seemed to me that the young and the old were the most important people. The people that were my age were making it happen. On the surface it looked as if the children were being indulged, but there was certainly no obnoxious behaviour. In fact, it was a joy to watch. In my world we have to be very careful when we indulge our children because they are apt to take advantage of the situation in a way that becomes obnoxious.*

Marie Wilson: I think that the difference lies in that relationship between authority and responsibility. We celebrated passages of life, which isn't done any more. The great token gesture is becoming old enough to go into a bar! In our society, as in all "primitive" societies, you celebrate your position within that society. Children are well aware of this progressive move through life. They look forward to it. But they know that when they move from one stage of life to another, a death has occurred for part of their life. They can look back, with whatever feeling, but now it's over and they're into something different. All of the changes were celebrated by all the people, marking the change—not only physical, but in terms of responsibility and rewards.

An example of this is the Nootka custom of young girls having to swim alone after they've come out of their first menstrual period from a very distant point in the ocean. The canoes leave the girl way out in the distance and she has to swim to the shore. The people stand in all their regalia, marking that it is important—her mother's people and her father's people. They cheer her on, sending out vibrations to give her strength when she is failing. And it is the oldest, wisest woman who puts the special robe on her.

TNC: *Do you see a revival of these rituals? They seem so important to human groups.*

Marie Wilson: Most of our customs became illegal under the authority of the missionaries. To get around the outlawing of feasting, we developed the idea of parties. The church had no objection to

Christmas parties, for instance. Incidentally, I reject this word "feast." The actual translation for what we do is "a gathering of the people." This meant feeding and housing the witnesses, who are extremely important, and entertaining them for about two weeks. There was an abundance of food and activity. The function of the song and dance was to imprint their memories forever.

"I have had the awful feeling that when we are finished dealing with the courts and our land claims, we will then have to battle the environmentalists and they will not understand why."

TNC: *Many of us who are trying to reconnect with the land are realizing that what is needed is a regeneration of culture. Fundamental to this is dealing with the great spiritual emptiness that so many of us are experiencing. What we are seeking is a religion that connects us to the land. Many of us can't help but try to emulate the native people. But some people feel uncomfortable with this.*

Marie Wilson: It's too easy to take that approach to redeeming oneself. Essentially this is what non-Indians are looking for. We can say it's for the world, or it's for people, but really it's for self. I can't see it happening. Each of us springs from some original beginning. It would be uncomfortable for me to attempt to go to Africa and take up their tribal practices, though I could understand the purpose. I believe our shadows follow us, that we do not arrive in this world meaningless, that the child who is born brings things with her. The Gitksan believe this wholeheartedly. You know how a little child holds her hand like this? Every older Indian will say, "What have you brought for lunch today?" We believe that the child carries in her hands preparations for life from somewhere else.

Here again we have to talk about energy. It has nothing to do with anything mystic. It has to do with energy. I believe firmly that, coming from a long line of very strong women, I was literally born with this same strength. The energy of my great-grandmother, my grandmother and mother has exhibited itself in me, and I know which daughter of mine will follow me.

At the risk of sounding scornful or derogatory, I have to say that the Indian attitude toward the natural world is different from the environmentalists'. I have had the awful feeling that when we are finished dealing with the courts and our land claims, we will then have to battle the environmentalists and they will not understand why. I feel quite sick at this prospect because the environmentalists want these beautiful places kept in a state of perfection: to not touch them, rather to keep them pure. So that we can leave our jobs and for two weeks we can venture into the wilderness and enjoy this ship in a bottle. In a way this is like denying that life is happening constantly in these wild places, that change is always occurring. Human life must be there too. Humans have requirements and they are going to have to use some of the life in these places. I do believe that life does not need humans but, rather, humans do need the rest of life. We are very small within the structure.

TNC: *So you don't take a stewardship perspective to the land—in the sense that the land needs our protection?*

Marie Wilson: Oh, never! No, the land can do what it will with me. We cannot whip the waves back. When the waves come, they can strip the California beach of million dollar homes with one contemptuous wave.

I worry about some of the young people who have been apart from their tradition for a long time, particularly in the cities. They don't have this true connection and they are going to have to struggle back to it as hard as you are going to have to struggle.

TNC: *That's really what we have to do. Do you have any advice for non-Indian people who are struggling for their vision?*

Marie Wilson: In Gitksan society, before you became adult enough to take on responsibility and power, you went out alone. Alone, we search for our full potential. After fasting for days and going into the sweat lodge and the cold waters of the stream, whipping oneself with the Devil's Club, I imagine we were in a fine state of hallucination. We had visions, usually in the form of a creature, or an encounter with a natural resource like the sun. The intention was not necessarily to find the creature but rather our own full potential.

When people fast, their bodies are reverting to the survival mode of existence where only that which is absolutely necessary is being taken from the body itself. This is going back to the natural Gitksan: taking only what is required. Our territories are taken for need, not greed. We take creatures for need, never more than we can use. When the body is in this state, fasting is not at all painful. You are then able to reach this perception where smell, touch, taste take on a fresh sensitivity. Not only these things, but also an increased perception of my place, my home, my children. So, imagine what happened to our people when they fasted for days. They became so empty that they were like snow in the spring— melting water drips through the snow and it becomes porous. This must have been the condition they were in—ready to receive.

The Gitksan accepted their intelligence for what it was, as they accepted their wonderful bodies. This intelligence, the product of the balancing between female and male, was the bridge between the body and the spirit. They could step lightly between each because they had such use of both sides of their intelligence. They had wonderful spatial vision because they used it and because there was no guilt on either side.

TNC: *We have to rediscover this intelligence. My concern has been that non-Indian people have the tendency to think that we can have it all now; there it is, over there in that native culture, I'll just go and take it. We can't do that.*

Marie Wilson: That's right. There's no way non-Indian people can really understand the emotion, the sense of defeat and elation, the way we've had to change our attitudes as we learned. None of this shows up. This has taken thousands of years for us to come to this point.

TNC: *What do we do then? As people who are desperate for this meaning?*

Marie Wilson: You will have to go back in your own history, as many Gitksan have had to do. We are drowning in statistics and yet we are aching for this knowledge.

"If trapping can't continue, or the killing of whales, or hunting of deer—whatever—then you have to talk about the alternatives. Because what's happened with our people historically is that we've just been *told* we can't do it. That's how we've been treated. Nobody ever wants to sit down and talk about alternatives."

10

Working Together: Natives, Non-Natives And The Future

George Watts

A s land claims and self-determination for native peoples inch ever closer to reality in British Columbia, it is natural that the alliance between native peoples and non-native environmental groups—at times harmonious, at times uneasy—should come in for closer scrutiny. This was highlighted in 1985-86 during the sealing and fur-trapping controversy, where native groups and Greenpeace, for example, came into conflict. Native groups claimed that the ban on Canadian fur-trapping and export sought by Greenpeace and other animal rights groups was "cultural genocide" for native communities who depended on the fur trade for their economic survival.

On other issues, native and non-native have worked well together—for instance, in the case of Meares Island, one of Canada's westernmost islands which faces the Pacific Ocean across from the small town of Tofino, in British Columbia. For western Canadians, Meares Island became a household word in the early 1980s when Macmillan Bloedell Ltd.—one of Canada's largest timber companies—threatened to clearcut log it. Vehemently opposed by the Nuu Chah Nulth people (the traditional owners of Meares Island), the township of Tofino, environmentalists and a broad cross section of the public, the proposal to log the island was defeated after a protracted struggle, notable for the way in which natives and non-natives worked together in common cause. Meares Island was declared a Tribal Park in 1984 and remains today a place of astonishing beauty where original coastal old-growth dwarfs humankind.

George Watts, President of the Nuu Chah Nulth Tribal Council, was active *in the struggle to save Meares Island. Here, he talks pragmatically about what native self-government might look like in the event that native peoples are successful in their land claims and in achieving aboriginal self-government.*

The New Catalyst: *Now that land claims and self- government are becoming a reality for native nations, maybe we can take a look at some of the directions you're planning on taking for the future.*

A lot of non-native groups have given their support to native causes—land claims, and protection of different environmental areas—but they're wondering if their needs will be recognized once land claims are met and you have control over the areas in question. Will there be an opportunity for non-native people to have their voices heard on decision-making committees?

Several native people have told me that it's not my land and it's not my business. But when you consider that it's all of our children that are going to be involved in all of the land and the environment, it seems that the decisions will be for all of us to make. How are you going to take that into account?

George Watts: If you talk about the future, you have to look at the past first. Our past history tells us that we have a relationship with all living things. Having said that, you have to recognize that we've been subjected to a non-Indian education system which obviously has had an effect on our values. Some of our people have lost touch with some of the teachings which have been passed on for many generations, and you have to deal with that reality. The other reality is that our people are chasing economic security.

Despite that, what our people have said is that we're not trying to pass on a world that we determine for our children or our grandchildren; we're trying to pass on the *opportunity* for our children to decide for themselves what kind of world they'll have. But what we see is that, with the destruction of the world, its environment, and with the ever-increasing consumerism, we aren't leaving much of an opportunity for our children to decide, and the world is growing smaller and smaller.

So let's talk about Meares Island. Our fight for Meares Island is based on aboriginal title. What we're saying is that our ownership of land is in conflict with the form of ownership of non-Indian peoples. Our interests have got to be taken care of, and we've got to come to an agreement about how we're going to co-exist in this world. Now the present position of the people who traditionally owned Meares Island is that they would like to leave the trees standing on Meares Island. That's supported by the rest of the tribal bands who say that the descendants of Clayoquot and Ahousat tribes have got the right to make their choice. But to ask me—or the leadership of the Clayoquot or Ahousat bands—where Meares Island is going to be 50 years from now, I wouldn't answer that for you because that will be up to our children to decide.

We're not trying to convince people that our cause is the right cause. What we do is tell them how we feel. Unfortunately, other people haven't been as honest with us over the last 100 years, about how they feel. In the long run, if people were just a little more honest with one another in putting everything on the table, we would quickly discover that everything isn't mapped out. It isn't all cut and dried, in terms of saying who's going to have a certain say in what we're doing. We don't know how that's going to be. If we did, I suppose we could sign an agreement that'd be in effect for the next thousand years....

"If you're not going to be a commercial fisherman; if you're not going to be a trapper; or if you're not going to go out and kill whales—then, what *are* you going to do? Are we *all* going to live on macaroni?—We should talk about it!"

TNC: *You say we'll pass this on to our children fifty years from now. But then at some point along the line some people might say, "We need the jobs," or "We need the economy more than we need those forests,"—the same thing that's been happening for so long. Jobs and economic security are important nowadays. At the same time, the work that we've experienced together—all the environmental situations and native concerns—have brought about a different type of value system. While we can't do without money, we can take the material parts of what we've developed and align that closer with some spiritual values, maybe, where we hold these areas in trust as sacred areas for the future of all people.*

George Watts: But you don't pass on values by putting them into agreements. You pass values on by how you bring your children up. So you and I may believe that Meares Island should be preserved forever, and those are the values that we would teach our children. But we would be fools not to recognize that there are other families in this world who are bringing their children up exactly on the other side of the spectrum, with the value that if you can make a dollar, you should do it. If we don't recognize that that's how our value system is being passed on, then we end up losing— our values are never taken into consideration.

TNC: *An example of what I mean might be the seven million dollars allocated federally for native forest management on the reserves. There's been a program to develop 75 reserves of the Nuu Chah Nulth people for timber-harvesting. Yet I don't really think that many of the forestry practices that have been evolving in the past 50-75 years, on the coast here especially, are very positive ones. The alder seems to be an important wood for your people for smoking fish; but forestry practices today involve cutting that down, eradicating it. What do you think about that kind of program?*

George Watts: As far as the forestry program is concerned, it's not true that it's all for harvesting. We accepted money on the basis that we would *plan* the forestry resource use. It might not necessarily mean cutting it down. In fact a lot of our plans have got nothing to do with cutting trees down.

TNC: *That's reassuring. At the Offshore Alliance of Aboriginal Nations Conference in 1986, a professor of political science from the University of British Columbia suggested a joint strategy approach in the use of land: committees with representatives of both nations sitting together. But people in Toronto might be making the decisions about what's going to happen in our forests here. Local representation today is missing. Will local people have the opportunity to offer ideas about the development of these land areas?*

George Watts: The end-result will have a lot to do with how the Indian people are treated in the process. If there's an indication from the larger society that they are talking about co-existing, then I think you're going to see a reciprocal attitude coming from native people. But if there continues to be a push against Indian people and we continue to be more isolated from the larger society, then that's exactly what will happen: Indian people will turn inward on themselves, and say, "Well, we tried to live and work with other people, and all we've ever got is the shit end of the stick!" For instance, if there's an agreement sometime down the road, how that agreement will be implemented will have a lot to do with how we were treated during the process.

TNC: *Maybe we can all learn from that how to respect and deal with each other better. I can see how that had its detrimental effects in the past. Now, though, there's an awful lot of support for native people and a lot of respect from a great deal of society. In fact, the Iroquois Nations' book of the Great Law—the six nations Confederacy from the Mohawk, New York, area—in the 1400s laid out some fantastic laws about how people can work together in peace.*

George Watts: Part of the American constitution is based on that.

TNC: *Yes. And people are appreciating all this knowledge you have kept alive for so long, and are looking toward your people for guidance.*

At the same time, we have to look at how we can all learn in developing the land. Like you said, it is a smaller world, and we're having a lot of problems with conservation. The fish and the deer, and a lot of other wildlife and habitat have been reduced to a fraction of original levels. And it's affecting everyone. We'll all have to work that out. And I don't think that the old ways, in a lot of situations—say, trapping, or some hunting—can continue in terms of harvesting at original levels.

George Watts: The history of the world is never fixed. If trapping can't continue, or the killing of whales, or hunting of deer—whatever—then you have to talk about the alternatives. Because what's happened with our people historically is that we've just been *told* we can't do it. That's how we've been treated. Nobody ever wants to sit down and talk about alternatives. For instance, the trappers up north and the fur ban in Europe: everybody had their say about it *except* for the people who were affected. What about talking to *them* and asking *them* how they feel, and what the alternatives are to what they were doing?

But the alternative is welfare, or becoming a drunk. The alternative is not acceptable. I suggest that you plan, and you know what the alternatives are when the need arises. So if we say there are too few deer now and the Indians can't hunt deer for food any more, then I say to you: what is the alternative? Because if there's no meaningful alternative on the table, then chaos is the alternative. If you're not going to be a commercial fisherman; if you're not going to be a trapper; or if you're not going to go out and kill whales—then what *are* you going to do? Are we *all* going to live on macaroni?—We should talk about it!

TNC: *You once said to the President of Macmillan Bloedell [one of the largest timber companies in British Columbia], at a shareholder's meeting that he could "tell Big Business that they have nothing to fear if government will negotiate land claims." Is your approach going to be similar to the way the corporations have operated out here, in their very abstract way of deciding the future of local people's lives? What kind of things can industry expect from you as far as timber is concerned, for example?*

George Watts: Let's talk about a land claims settlement dealing with timber. If we were not prepared to talk to non-Indian people, including the loggers and business, about how we would implement this settlement, whatever it may be, then I think we would be doing to them exactly what was done to us. That's not our philosophy. So when I say that at a Macmillan Bloedell meeting, I mean it. I would intend that we would sit down with Macmillan Bloedell and other companies in our traditional area, and we would talk about the long-term effect of whatever it is that our people are going to do. And we would sit down with the IWA—the International Woodworkers Association—and talk about the long-term effect on their workers. And we would try to work out something that's as close as possible to what's agreeable to all of us—that we can *all* live with. I'm not saying that I would in any way guarantee that their plans would be carried out. But I would sit down with them.

TNC: *Are mining rights going to be a part of your land claims?*

George Watts: Well, we don't say things like "mining rights" or "logging rights" or anything like that. We just say rights, period. When we talk about our lands, we're talking about what *we* see in those lands. Not what anybody else sees. So if there's a mine there, and some band believes in mining, then there *will* be a mine there. If the band says, "No, we don't want to dig the earth up," then there won't be a mine.

TNC: *One of the strongest ideas lately is that of farming the forests. But I wonder if we can really* farm *the forests?*

George Watts: Well you can farm it as long as you understand it. But it isn't the natural way. In the Meares Island court case, the lawyer kept on saying that the trees would be back 80 years from now, and it was nonsense that people wouldn't be able to walk in the forest. Well, walking in the forest where the trees are spaced ten feet away from each other, exactly the same distance in the north and south direction as in the east and west direction, that is not the same as walking in a forest that was put there by other forces!

But forests can be farmed as long as you understand that that's what you're doing. You only have to go to Sweden to see well-farmed forests. But that's all they are. They *are* farms. They're no different than a corn farm or a wheat farm. The Swedish people, better than anyone else, have been able to demonstrate to the greatest extent possible, that it *is* possible to do forest farming by mechanical means—without chemicals. But people in Sweden don't go for a walk in the forest farms as a walk in nature!

"Every environmental question I have seen in this world has come back down to that. That you'd have to have a philosophical shift, to have less consumerism and leave more of the world intact."

TNC: *Would there be any possibility of maintaining a forest by harvesting some of those trees for specialty markets, with your own mills, and continuing to do it the way you did it before?*

George Watts: The things you talk about are ideals, but you can't deal in a micro-situation. Let's say you talk about doing forestry in a different fashion, taking only one tenth of the trees that we presently take. And we try to get a higher market value out of it. You do that and you're affecting world markets. If you sell a thousand dollars worth of nice cedar, then what do you do with the thousand dollars? You buy goods off another country that's shipping goods in. So it isn't just a matter of saying that we're going to cut just one tenth of the trees. There are many other things that are affected by those decisions. If people would quit buying so many television sets from Japan, then you wouldn't need so much money selling your goods out of the country. That's really what it comes down to. Even in the most remote and under-developed countries, it's still based on what people create and what they consume.

So when you talk about how resources are used, it isn't just as simple as saying we should cut fewer trees, or we should not be so profit-oriented. Maybe we shouldn't. But it goes far beyond that, to changing societies, making a major philosophical shift in the way this world's going. Because greed is a philosophy which has been in existence for thousands of years; and it's spread all over this world.

In politics, it seems you can't even convince *local* people that they should start thinking about it. You can't convince people at a provincial level, you can't convince people at a national level. So what the hell are the chances of convincing people on a *global* scale that there should be a philosophical shift in the direction the world's going? Every environmental question I have seen in this world has come back down to that. That you'd have to have a philosophical shift, to have less consumerism and leave more of the world intact.

TNC: *Maybe legislation has to be introduced...?*

George Watts: But how are you going to enact legislation when you can't even elect a government? Not even a *compromise* government, let alone a government that would bring in those types of legislation.

TNC: *Many people are hoping that land claims will stall enviromental destruction for a little while...*

George Watts: There's no doubt that land claims will stall that type of destruction, but people shouldn't put all their eggs into one basket!

"Bioregionalism is striking at the very base of our chaos: our lack of place.   As lost souls, or individuals, we're searching desperately for ways to answer this survival need. Consensus has been a natural outgrowth. Part of the power of the bioregional movement has grown out of its success with consensus."

11

Consensus And Community
Caroline Estes

Building cultures that are sustainable over the long term requires us to pay as much attention to how we do things as to what we do. Making decisions together—whether in a single-issue environmental group, a neighborhood, or a visionary "shadow government"—can either build, or break, community. Casting aside the old adage that "the end justifies the means," bioregional activists have focussed careful attention upon process.

Caroline Estes is a founding member of Alpha Farm intentional community in Oregon, and an accomplished practitioner and teacher of facilitation and consensus. She successfully facilitated the first three North American Bioregional Congresses—the bi-annual, week-long gatherings of over 150 disparate people from numerous regions of Turtle Island and beyond—with the result that consensus is now firmly entrenched as the decision-making process by which the Congress makes its formally agreed upon statements. In this interview, she outlines the history and methodology of consensus, and its importance in creating collective unity.

The New Catalyst: *Consensus seems to be catching on in a range of groups, from small households up to large gatherings such as the North American Bioregional Congress. Is that your impression, too?*

Caroline Estes: Yes. In at least the western culture, the idea of individual rights has been very strong over many years and we're now seeing the results of too much reliance on that, and the need to come together to make a unified statement or action. And consensus is clearly the most efficient and effective method of doing that, honoring many different sides of the question which might be obscured in other forms of decision-making. It gives everybody the power to be part of the process.

TNC: *Can you give an example?*

Caroline Estes: Yes, I'll take my own home as an example: all of our decisions are made consensually. There is a lot of tension around a lot of subjects, and sometimes it's hard to get to them. For instance, let's take the vegetarian issue which many people are dealing with these days. In our particular case, we faced this both ethically and from the practical point of view of money. We drew out from every person that was participating in this decision, their personal place on how they felt about their diet, the impact of their diet on the world—things that you normally don't get into in a regular decision-making process. We found that we could honour each other in our different places *and* come to a decision, in our case eating vegetarian with additions of milk and cheese and eggs, eliminating red meat and occasionally adding fish or chicken. Now this did not meet any one person's total expectations. But, in hearing every person's point of view, we were able to satisfy everyone well enough to feel good about the diet that we have at Alpha Farm—which runs from 20 to 30 people.

TNC: *What would you say, then, is the objective of consensus?*

Caroline Estes: To find decisions together that everyone can agree with, feel comfortable with, and particpate in—not just have someone else do it. This is where I have always been uncomfortable with Robert's Rules of Order kinds of decision-making where, yes, you can come to a decision, and the majority has clearly carried, but it's *their* decision, it's not *our* decision.

TNC: *Can you tell us briefly how consensus works in your experience?*

Caroline Estes: My understanding of consensus comes from an investigation of two streams. One is the Society of Friends who have practiced it for about 300 years, and the other is from the native traditions where they've practiced it for maybe millenia.

Consensus is where a question is asked (and the question must be phrased positively, not negatively), and then everyone who is there speaks their mind, shares their truth, gives their opinion—and out of all of the sharing, there starts to emerge a common answer to the question that moves the group to a decision. An important point is that you must be *present* to take part in consensus, there is no absentee voting. Depending upon whether or not you have someone who is serving the group as a facilitator, it can go quicker or slower. If a facilitator is there, they can be paying more attention to this gathering agreement, and possibly move the group ahead a little quicker.

At some point a decision is self-evident. At that point, it needs to be stated, and a search made of the group to see whether the decision has indeed answered all of the various questions that people have, and has satisfied them to the point that they can agree. It does not mean unanimity, that everybody is in absolute, total alignment. That is something that I think we reach very seldom. But in consensus it is fairly easy to arrive at a place of unity which people can get behind, and then move forward together.

Now it is possible that, for some people, what is being decided is wrong, or they have not yet felt comfortable enough with it to join it. At that point, people are called upon to say that they are stepping aside from this decision. They need to be minuted or registered as having stepped aside, so that they no longer have to participate in the action that falls out from the decision. It does *not* mean that they are holding the group up. In my particular experience, I find that if two or more people start stepping aside, we have not done enough work to arrive at the very best decision. And there are those very few and far between cases where someone in the group has the very clear understanding that they, at that particular moment, have more wisdom and light than everyone else, and they have the responsibility of holding the group from moving ahead. This is what we call blocking.

"Consensus is where a question is asked, and then everyone who is there speaks their minds... and out of all of the sharing, there starts to emerge a common answer..."

TNC: *Is it true that this is not frequently used in true consensus?*

Caroline Estes: In my 25-30 years of being involved with consensual groups, I've seen it less than a dozen times. And that's stretching. It's very rare that any of us has the audacity to think that we have more wisdom than the collected wisdom of the group. And when those occasions occur, it is very difficult for us to take that stand. You must be *terribly* sure. Not so much intellectually, but at that feeling, or gut level that says, "This is wrong. I am not able to let these friends make this mistake, and I have a responsibility to stop them." It's very difficult.

TNC: *You spoke about the role of the facilitator. Could you expand on that a little more?*

Caroline Estes: In my experience so far, the facilitator—who is just that: a person who has the role of making easy the movement towards decision—is fairly crucial at this particular time in the emergence of consensus as a decision-making process. We are not yet all good at taking part in meetings on an equal basis. We have not been trained to do that, to have full ease at sharing our thinking and our feelings. So in a meeting, if there is one person who basically steps out of the content that's being discussed, and pays attention only to the process, it greatly facilitates the discussion and the ability of everyone to take part. Because that person is making sure that everyone's bit of the truth is being added to the collective. This is a nudge for people to start realizing that their truth is really important. And it is also a person or a place that helps some people who may have been used to talking more than their proportionate share to understand the need to have a little bit more control over that and to allow space for people who *aren't* used to talking. It's someone who simply watches the process and makes sure the people stay on track.

TNC: *Do you see it as an interim institution, before we can do this without facilitators, or is it something that we really need to have on a permanent basis?*

Caroline Estes: I would say any group of over 30 needs a facilitator. Simply because it's hard to facilitate yourself. Under 30 I would hope that, as we move forward with the use of consensus and the honoring of each person's position, we become so trained and sensitized to the understanding of truth that we could indeed facilitate ourselves and wouldn't need a facilitator.

TNC: *This is a worthy ideal. However, many peoples' experience with using consensus has been little short of disasterous. Consensus has been blamed as the problem—I'm speaking here, say, about political parties' attempts to use consensus—and frequently the comment is made that consensus can't work in impersonal or large gatherings. What's your response to that?*

Caroline Estes: I don't see any particular reason why consensus can't work in any face-to-face situation. So long as there's a common purpose, even if people don't know each other, there is no reason why consensus can't be used. The largest group I ever saw was 5,000, and it was a very powerful group that was brought together with great unity. This was the free speech movement in Berkeley. There were some pretty stiff differences sometimes, but still the commonness of their goals made it fairly easy. It was an awesome experience. I think that when people get into trouble sometimes in large groups, it is because they really are there for different purposes.

It's true that consensus has often failed in groups and my experience of this is that true consensus has not been understood. It grew out of the late 50s/early 60s experience of large groups of people operating with something like consensus where the word caught on, and the power of the process was so great that they took it back to their own individual groups and they scattered around the country, without understanding where it came from, what its basis in *fact* is, and how much you have to work to unify the group to be sure it has a common purpose *before* you make any decisions. Part of what I have been doing over the last four or five years is going around and cleaning up disaster areas by bringing forth again the whole basis for consensus: where it comes from, and how you *must* practice it.

In one sense consensus is much more than a decision-making process, in that it requires us to be the very best that we can be. It does not let us keep all our shortcomings unchallenged.

"Both Abalone and Clamshell Alliances used consensus. The police just could not understand how 3,000 people could make decisions in five minutes that *they* couldn't make!"

TNC: *Could you give us an idea of the history of consensus?*

Caroline Estes: Historically, there was a man named George Fox who started the Society of Friends in England, 300 years ago. Growing out of his very deeply held and resonating feeling with many other people that there is that of God in every person, came the idea that, when you are making a decision, you should listen to *all* of it. And it should all be incorporated into the decision. If there were people who didn't agree, and that which was of God in them was saying "No," then you needed to listen to that. They called this the sense of the meeting. The word "consensus" is not a Quaker term.

The sense of the meeting is just that: that out of the meeting to make decisions, came a sense of the correctness of how you proceed. That was then minuted, and on that rested the actions that followed. That's one direction that has come forth pretty much unchanged through the years.

The other side has to do with the native people in the United States— and that's all I've done research on so far. The way they made decisions was by a number of forms of consensus. In one tribe, all of the men would sit in a circle and all of the women would sit in a circle behind them. And the decision was made by the collective of everyone there. They never made a decision without that completeness.

TNC: *How does this compare historically with Robert's Rules of Order and that whole tradition?*

Caroline Estes: When Colonel Robert wrote his Rules of Order—it was during the gold-rush chaos of San Fransisco in 1867—it actually was a gigantic step forward in group decision-making. Prior to that, each group sort of made up its own rules of procedure. It was a great step forward because everyone's rights were spelled out very clearly: it accomodated the minority by giving them certain power; and it gave the groups an ability to move forward in an orderly fashion, with everyone knowing the rules.

But Robert's Rules of Order can be manipulated. The parliamentarian is the strongest person in a Robert's Rules of Order group. And today we recognize that we can no longer have majorities and minorities; we need collective unity.

TNC: *How does consensus help the process of forming communities, do you think—both intentional communities intending to live together, as well as peoples' less coherent attempts at forming community?*

Caroline Estes: The whole process requires knowing each other, exposing our truth. And to the extent that we do that, we build community. It's an integral part of the consensual process, because you *have* to share that. If not, you are short-changing the group. Completely.

So let's say you're a neighborhood group, and not an intentional community. Just the act of being in a group that is using consensus means that the neighborhood gets to know each other as individuals much better than just acting on a set of rules. Many of us have backgrounds that allow us to have very different perceptions of different aspects of the question. And as we expose our backgrounds, we become more whole to other people. It's this slow recognition that we need to know each other that seems to me to be very helpful.

"The basis of consensus, the ground on which it rests, is trust. Without trust, consensus really hobbles along. But it also engenders trust. It's sort of a circle."

TNC: *Many intentional communities have fallen apart over the last decade or two, after many different attempts at coming together. Alpha Farm is one intentional community that's managed to stick together. Is that because of consensus? And if so, can you tell us how it works within your community?*

Caroline Estes: I think consensus was absolutely crucial to how we began, in that we didn't know each other, and this was the process of coming to know each other. The basis of consensus, the ground on which it rests, is trust. Without trust, consensus really hobbles along. But it also engenders trust. It's sort of a circle. The more you do it, the more trust you build, and the larger the base on which you're resting. And the more you use it, the more trust you have, the more consensus is easy. Then what you do is easier, because the power behind unity is tremendous. I think Alpha Farm in the beginning would not have made it without consensus. Fortunately we had the process correctly in order. Some groups who came together did not, and did not understand how to use consensus, or the importance of parts of it, and therefore allowed what I would consider a manipulation of the process. But it's very difficult to manipulate a true consensual decision-making process. I've never really seen it happen.

TNC: *What about passing the skills of consensus on to children. What's your experience of that?*

Caroline Estes: I think it's a lot easier to advance the idea of consensus in households, which is basically where children of Friends learn. You don't necessarily need a facilitator, although it does help. In a few families I know, they took minutes at their family councils. And sometimes the children would go back and point out the minute to the adults! So it was a very empowering thing for children, and we don't have a lot of ways of empowering children specifically. Consensus obviously needs to be used with discretion among children—children don't always have all of the light completely grown in them—but to the degree that that starts evolving, the more it's brought into family council probably the better the family's inter- relationships. It's a way of starting to train people in our society to feel empowered, and to be OK with empowering other people; that it's not scarey; it's their right, and it's their right to empower others.

TNC: *So if you had a recipe for building sustainable cultures, what would the primary ingredients be?*

Caroline Estes: Well, real love and respect. Consensus could be a very important part of bringing about those two rather vital ingredients. I do think the more feminine traits need to be integrated in a much more equal way in any society that we're going to evolve that is going to be sustainable. And it is true that consensus is a feminine form of decision-making: it is unifying, it is sharing, it is caring, it is non-dominant, it is empowering. This integration is going to be essential for our survival.

The civil rights movement and the anti-war movement had a tremendous amount of male domination—very large male egos in them. And the whole thrust of consensus and the feminine aspect to making these two movements work never got a full chance in them. That's not true today. I'm thinking now of the anti-nuclear groups which used a consensual process to arrive at their decisions. For example, the Clamshell Alliance against the Seabrook nuclear power plant in Concord, New Hampshire, numbered 3,000 people. And the power that was behind those groups! Those places are still closed. The police just could not understand how 3,000 people could make decisions in five minutes that *they* couldn't make! In nuclear issues, it's that survival factor that raises the consciousness of the need for unity.

My guess is that the bioregional movement is kind of the same thing. Bioregionalism is striking at the very base of our chaos: our lack of place. As lost souls, or individuals, we're searching desperately for ways to answer this survival need. Consensus has been a natural outgrowth. Part of the power of the bioregional movement has grown out of its success with consensus. There has not been the need for minorities to be putting forth their positions all the time. Which, if you look at parties or units of social movements, that's often been the technique that's done them in—all that back-biting. I'm watching the Green Party with interest to see whether or not they can get themselves together well enough to use consensus and recognize the power behind it. Once you have a unified decision, I'd suggest everyone get out of the way, because you can go a long way with *very* little!

"...one of the beauties of trying to develop a restoration ethic through a workforce is that working together provides people with a common experience and a lot of common experiential information.... I've found no more effective way of seeing these ideas arise in the hearts of more individuals than by this kind of shared work."

12

Salmon And Settler: Toward A Culture Of Reinhabitation

Freeman House

Many areas of the west have already been exploited and abandoned, leaving local people to cope with the aftermath. This situation has led, in turn, to the twin fundamental ideas of bioregionalism: reinhabitation and restoration—fundamental building blocks in the task of creating ecologically sustainable futures. Reinhabitation involves becoming native to a place, learning what its unique characteristics and needs might be, and what kinds of human activities it might support if we were to fit ourselves to the land, not require the land to bend to our demands. Equally, the restoration of damaged ecosystems is, for many, the real work of the future, requiring new sensibilities that most of us must learn from scratch.

In northern California's Mattole Valley, a long-time haven for reinhbitants, an eight year old restoration project is now beginning to pay dividends—both for the watershed and the consciousness of the people. There, a small band of dedicated people decided in 1981 to launch an ambitious attempt to restore the river's salmon population, depleted owing to logging and subsequent siltation. The project has developed into a life's work for many of those involved, and has led to a unique body of watershed information and local action which includes local high school students. Freeman House, one of the prime movers of the Mattole Restoration Council, was one of those who conceived the project while with the Planet Drum Foundation in San Fransisco. Not content with the theory of reinhabitation alone, he felt he had to put it into practice personally. Here he explains how the Mattole people have approached such restoration and the *philosophy behind their work.*

The New Catalyst: *Can you briefly describe the Mattole Valley for us?*

Freeman House: It's 306 square miles in area, with no large population centers. What's unique about the valley is that it's remote, hard to get into and, until very recently, it was self-sufficient to the degree that it still operated as a resource base. That included timber harvesting and cattle and sheep production. For maybe ten years now, timber production has not been a big item of income, because it's gone. And what is being cut is being cut by non-local crews who are brought in from outside the valley. It's getting harder and harder to make a living at ranching—the price differentiation between feed and medicines and the price of meat has become too much of a crunch. As a result of both of those things, a lot of subdivision has gone on in the last 20 years and there's been a large influx of back-to-the-land people, starting in about 1968. So the population of the place has tripled to about two thousand right now. A lot of the people are largely on 40 and 80 acre parcels, on steep lands, cut-over, and in many cases poorly regenerated. There are tremendous erosion problems.

About ten years ago, a very few of the new settlers who were in the habit of talking to the older residents began to suspect that the native King Salmon run there was on the verge of extinction.

"...91 per cent of the old growth coniferous forests—all the forests of commercial value—are gone, all taken out in the last 40 years. There's nine percent of the original forest left."

TNC: *For what reasons?*

Freeman House: Erosion problems due to the poor timber harvest practices. Particularly, silt was coming off the hillsides and filling up all the pools and spawning areas in the river. It wasn't apparent to the general public that this was happening. The local tradition was still to poach—to take fish for local consumption. It was not a popular idea that the salmon run was disappearing. What our people knew that most people didn't was that this is one of the five or six native Chinook (or King—we call them Kings for future reference) salmon runs in California.

TNC: *Can you give us any facts to show the degeneration of the forest resource as well as the salmon?*

Freeman House: Our recent figures show that 91% of the old growth coniferous forests—all the forests of commercial value—are gone, all taken out in the last 40 years. There's nine percent of the original forest left. Of that, only one third, or three percent, is available for any kind of reserve status. When we published our maps none of it had any protection at all. Since that time, people have become very active and, at this point, two percent of the original forest (which is two thirds of what is now available for reserve status) does have some protection.

TNC: *And do you have any statistics about the re- growth?*

Freeman House: We're developing those. That's the next step in the process. Hopefully we'll be able to develop treatment toward massive reforestation of the Mattole. The historical situation is that no-one was required to re-plant after harvest until 1975. By that time most of the harvest had already been accomplished. What that means is that there is no second rotation. California has been operating on the fiction of sustained yield for all these years, and we've been able to demonstrate now that in the Mattole—which I suspect is not untypical for private lands— we're 30 to 50 years away from a second rotation.

TNC: *What kind of a climate are we talking about here?*

Freeman House: It's extreme northern California climate: winter wet and summer dry. It's wetter in the winter and drier in the summer than most parts of California. So we get tremendous rainfall in the winter which, with steep slopes, makes the river very flashy and creates erosion problems.

TNC: *OK, so we were talking about the salmon?*

Freeman House: Yes, it was the demise of the salmon that first gave people the impulse toward restoration. And also the understanding—which no-one had known how to treat—that if the resource base was gone as a way of livelihood there, how were people going to continue to live in the place? The only other options—tourism and light industry, over which there was no way to control the input or the output—seemed less desireable.

People began an effort of restoring the salmon runs largely as an effort of the heart. That then grew into a realization that we could adopt the goal of restoring the place to its historical levels of health and productivity, and that that was best done—and could possibly *only* be done—by the people who lived there. No-one else is going to have any interest, in the first place, and they're the only people who can do it cost-effectively. You can imagine the federal government coming in and spending millions and millions—possibly billions—of dollars, but you can't imagine the Mattole becoming a priority operation. We've demonstrated over and over again that people with the local information, living nearby the problems, with a local understanding of the problems, are able to do the same work for perhaps as little as a tenth the cost.

We've pursued our restoration goals by four paths: salmon enhancement, erosion control, reforestation and education. Over eight years, our numbers have grown from a handful of people to probably 20 who are committed to the work and the ideas in a full way, and maybe 100 people who make some part of their income from it, and probably another couple of hundred people who support it, either monetarily or by inviting restoration people on to their land to see what can be done.

"We've pursued our restoration goals by four paths: salmon enhancement, erosion control, reforestation and education."

TNC: *What kinds of activities are we talking about here?*

Freeman House: Showcase activities: the annual hatchbox program where we go out and capture native stock, take the eggs, incubate them, and then release them back into the wild. We use little hatchbox systems which are backyard incubators: they're always located near someone's home so they can be checked daily; they're all very low- tech, gravity-feed, no electricity involved.

TNC: *Have you had success with this program?*

Freeman House: Yes. We tend to plant the fish in streams where the fish are absent. So that when you see fish in that location, you can pretty much assume they're yours. We also have been doing carcass counts and population estimates during the spawning season every year consistently for eight years, applying the same formulas and the same techniques. And we've seen the numbers probably double in the time we've been working. But you have to understand that the numbers of fish we started with were even lower than we thought. Perhaps fewer than 500 individual King Salmon using the rivers when we started, and we didn't know that. So they may have more than doubled.

TNC: *Do you know what the previous number might have been? Was this a burgeoning stream?*

Freeman House: Well, the Department of Fish & Wildlife estimated in 1964 that there was habitat for 36,000 pairs of salmon. But they didn't count the fish.

So that's been succesful, but as soon as you get into salmonid enhancement, you recognize in a real concrete way the indicator species nature of the beast. And you realize that you can't restore natural systems by putting fish back in the water. All you're doing is building yourself into a permanent interfering sort of relationship with natural systems. We weren't looking to do that, to providing ourselves with jobs forever.

TNC: *So what did you do instead?*

Freeman House: We realized that we had to consider the entire watershed. And salmon guided us to that. If we couldn't think about the stream restoring itself to something like its original structure, we may as well cop to being careerists, rather than bioregionalists of the heart, as some of the key people are.

One interesting aspect is the experience we've had demonstrating that watersheds are unclaimed territories. Often all the information that you need to understand watershed systems is available *somewhere*, but it's almost never organized into that context. All of the residents are on record as a county, in aphabetical order, for the whole county—*not* as a watershed. All the forest maps are for the state as a whole, or for one seven and a half minute quad. It takes six 15 minute quadrangle maps to construct a map of this watershed of 300 square miles. And it takes a tremendous amount of work to re- organize that information. Once you do that, however, you're in a position of power, in that, as watershed residents, you are the only people who have that information. You can then demonstrate the importance of it. Before you have it, you can only *talk* about the importance of it, and it's easy to brush you off.

We think of our constituency as the residents and landowners in the watershed. So any time we publish anything, it goes out to every address on that list.

TNC: *What benefits are there in such a re- formulation?*

Freeman House: It's a powerful political tool. And it promises to be a powerful tool for consciousness. What we've found in real life is that people readily accept watershed consciousness on a smaller scale. Almost anybody we talk to can relate to themselves as a person who lives near the creek, and the watershed of the creek they live on. When you ask them to extend their sense of responsibility to the larger riverine watershed, for most people it's still difficult. But I feel that if we keep providing them with information, over the course of the years that's going to become second nature to a large enough portion of the population that it will make a difference.

On another level, politically, the watershed information gives you real ammunition to deal with political entities: federal, state, and county. Often it's simply a matter of embarrassment—that you know more than they do. Sometimes it's more a technical matter of having reorganized the information into a format that makes managerial sense. And none of the official entities have yet bothered to do that. An awful lot of this information is emerging through the grass-roots. There's an awful lot of old-growth mapping, like we did, being done in various places.

TNC: *How have you gone about planning the restoration work?*

Freeman House: One of our failings has been that, because none of this information is available in a watershed context, and because information about the degradation is not available *at all*—rather it's ignored—we've been forced into a position of attacking the degradation of the watershed on a kind of hit-and-miss basis. In the past we have selected something as important because somebody who lived near it thought it was important and was willing to devote the next year to fixing it. We haven't made too many mistakes that way. But it hasn't been entirely satisfactory.

"Watershed information gives you real ammunition to deal with political entities: federal, state, and county. Often it's simply a matter of embarrassment—that you know more than they do."

But what we have done is decided what was the most important element to attack next—this landslide, or that streambank erosion problem, or a fish ladder on a culvert, or a road that needed to be put to bed—again depending on what kind of passion and interest there was around it.

TNC: *So your approach has been identifying the trouble spots, prioritizing them, and then tackling them as best you can?*

Freeman House: Yes. What I'm proud of about our efforts in the past is that we have always decided among ourselves what was the most important thing to attack next and then gone and sought money for it. Rather than researching the sources of money and then deciding what we had that fit into that. I think that's important to a community's sense of self-reliance and control.

TNC: *Are we talking here of voluntary activity—the labour component? Or modest pay? How does it work?*

Freeman House: Whenever possible we've attempted to find the money to pay people, feeling that until the place is a resource base again, this is the proper economic base for the place. We're lucky that, in the state of California, that consciousness is growing, especially around the issue of salmon. And for the last seven years, there have been small amounts of money available in the state of California that are let out on a contract basis to do this kind of work: about a million dollars a year.

About four million dollars worth of proposals are received. So it's a very competitive thing. We've got about half of our money that way; the other half from various sources: private foundations, local donations, fund-raising efforts of various kinds, appeals through a newsletter. So we've come to the point in the last couple of years where we're paying workers somewhere between $100 and $2,000 a year. Eight years ago, almost all the work was volunteer.

Another aspect of our work that we have no way of monitoring is that we provide as much information as we can about how people on their own places might be doing this work themselves: information about gully-repair, revegetation, road-problems and road-building. Sometime soon we hope to be able to develop a handbook around these items, called something like "Erosion Control and Reforestation for the Mattole." Right now we're doing a survey of point sources of erosion in the entire watershed, from aerial photographs. People are then going out to them and trying to come up with rough prescriptions. We're attempting to do the same thing with forest regeneration.

TNC: *Has the common interest that exists in a watershed gelled into a significant force?*

Freeman House: It has happened to a certain extent. People who live in the Mattole Valley expect there to be people talking this language. And it is part of their language. But one of the beauties of trying to develop a restoration ethic through a workforce is that working together provides people with a common experience and a lot of common experiential information. That allows a level of communication that I don't know how to get at by any other means—not by the written word, not by videotape, not through tax-breaks. I've found no more effective way of seeing these ideas arise in the hearts of more individuals than by this kind of shared work.

TNC: *So through this work you're building a culture of reinhabitation in a real sense.*

Freeman House: Yes, exactly. And people will begin to look at their own daily activities which is a big problem in this very erosive watershed. Every one of these 40 acre homesteaders feels it's necessary to have their own private road. Many of them come directly from the city; they don't know anything about building roads, and just punch one in. They find the first winter destroys it, and then they go back and do it again! But once they've worked at repairing a failed road, or putting a road to bed, or sizing and installing an appropriate culvert, they're beginning to understand some processes that are really a part of their everyday life. To the degree that you've been able to pay them for that, many of them are absolutely delighted, because it tends to be pleasurable work.

TNC: *The Restoration Council is also involved in education, too, isn't it?*
Freeman House: Yes, this is a very important aspect of our work—work of more than one generation. Petrolia School (with a population of 16 students) has been operating as an alternative watershed high school for five years now in a valley with no other high school. Restoration activities serve as laboratories for earth and life sciences. Sometimes the students form part of the workforce, and often (amazingly) use the money to pay their teachers. In the elementary public school, there is now an entire generation which has released fish into the wild every year of their primary schooling. The same school has also adopted the policy of *local* environmental studies as part of the curriculum, and two of the three teachers are very active. These kids will know their birds and trees and fish!

"One of the beauties of trying to develop a restoration ethic through a workforce is that working together provides people with a common experience and a lot of common experiential information. That allows a level of communication that I don't know how to get at by any other means."

TNC: *Can you give a quick prescription for people who are living in watersheds that have been degraded for whatever reasons, and want to restore them? How would you go about it?*

Freeman House: Can we assume that these watersheds have salmon streams in them? That's easy because it turns out that no-one is antagonistic to salmon. If you can make people aware that salmon is what you're helping, almost no- one can say no.   The first thing to do is to learn as much about the state of the salmon run in your river, and as much as you can about the real potential of the watershed. If you discover that the run is far below the potential, then you begin trying to determine why. I would guess that in more than half the cases it's going to be erosional problems. In other cases it's going to be pollution problems, or maybe cultural problems. There are places where local harvest can go beyond the carrying capacity. Try to determine that.

Find access to experts. Do not put down expertise; there's a lot of it out there, it's tremendously valuable, and I would be willing to guess that anyone who persistently starts looking for technical assistance from experts, either on the academic level or even in state and provincial and federal agencies, will sooner or later find someone who'll jump at the chance to get out there with people on the ground and help. We've found that to be true over and over and over again. And now we've got a little bit famous, and we get experts coming at us just before we need them! Also, don't be discouraged!

TNC: *And, presumably, build up a sense of community around your watershed?*

Freeman House: Well, I'd see that as the true goal of restoration work. In a way, the consciousness that you pursue through restoration work is at least equal in importance to the actual restoration. Because you can fix something, or you can plant a tree, or stop a point source of siltation, and walk away from it and there's no reason not to assume that somebody's not going to come right behind you and mess it up. So if you're not changing the consciousness along with the restoration work, you're doing some sort of make-work, band-aid thing.

(The Mattole Restoration Council can be contacted at: Box 160, Petrolia, CA 95558. One of their resources is a watershed map comparing old-growth, 1947-1988.)

"...what we're trying to do is create an economy as if the Earth really mattered. Bioregional strategies will not necessarily be able to offer jobs like IBM can. We have to look at longer term strategies with more spiritual, natural and community kinds of rewards."

13

Breaking Free:
Building Bioregional
Economies

Susan Meeker-Lowry

The global economy penetrates the furthest reaches of Third and First Worlds alike. Disregarding the bounds of nature as much as the differences of culture, international capital has made drones of the greater part of humanity, enslaving it into a pathological dependency upon distant citadels of power and the arbitrary motions of stockmarkets and multinational companies. Breaking free from this bondage, empowering our local communities once again, is the ultimate challenge of the bioregional endeavor. And, since only a change of lifestyle makes such liberation from the all-consuming "system" possible, it is also a subversive—and therefore risky—act, at whatever level one chooses to take it on.

Susan Meeker-Lowry is the editor of Catalyst, a newsletter of the Institute for Gaean Economics in Vermont which focuses on investing in social change, and author of Economics As If The Earth Really Mattered: A Catalyst Guide to Socially Conscious Investing (New Society Publishers, 1988). She is also active with the bioregional economics committee of the North American Bioregional Congress. Here she outlines several strategies that can be used to work toward economic liberation at both local and global levels.

The New Catalyst: *One of the main problems in the world today is that local economies are controlled by large, often multinational, corporations—a situation that disempowers people, causing unemployment and environmental degradation. How does a bioregional economics propose to change this* *situation?*

Susan Meeker-Lowry: For a bioregional economics to work, we need to develop comprehensive plans for each bioregion based on the needs of the people and the place, and concrete, practical strategies to get control out of the hands of the large corporations and into the hands of the people.

TNC: *What do you see as the essential characteristics of a bioregional economy?*

Susan Meeker-Lowry: The principles of bioregional economies are co-operation for the good of the whole; respect for all living beings, including and especially non-human forms; an awareness of how natural systems work and how humans might fit in with natural systems so that, rather than trying to shape those systems to fit our needs, we would be more integrated into nature—all of our plans and businesses would have to be integrated into the Earth context rather than trying to shift the Earth to fit us. Self-reliance is really important, too—being able to support ourselves as much as possible with resources both human and natural from the *region* rather than, for example, living in Vermont and depending on the distant rainforest for various different "necessities." Obviously it means looking at our lifestyles, and the kinds of things that we have come to expect growing up in these times; we can, and really must, begin to do without a lot of these things. We need to adopt some old ethics that our grandparents probably tried to pound into our heads and which we ignored, like "waste not want not," or "a stitch in time saves nine,"—all those boring little things that are so practical.

TNC: *You have written that we need economies that are accountable to human beings and the Earth? How will we recognize such economies?*

Susan Meeker-Lowry: There won't be a lot of pollution, or a lot of people sleeping in the streets. There would be people employed at jobs that they consciously choose; whether in their own business or someone else's, they'd work not just because they need to pay the rent, but because they care about the work that they do. The majority of people in this country work so that they can spend money when they're not working. Work needs to be a much more integrated part of our lives, an expression of who we are, rather than a means to an end.

Our whole educational system would be different, with kids being taught what it means to be human as a species, not just human as a social being. They would learn about the natural environment and become excited about this, and teachers would keep alive the mystery and the magic that we feel as kids, rather than consciously trying to snuff it out which is what they seem to do in the schools today.

We won't feel as pressured. Life will be more of a celebration instead of a trial. Even when we have suffering, we will have the support of community to make it bearable. Community is what really makes life worthwhile anyway.

"The principles of bioregional economies are co-operation for the good of the whole; respect for all living beings, including and especially non-human forms; an awareness of how natural systems work and how humans might fit in with natural systems so that, rather than trying to shape those systems to fit our needs, we would be more integrated into nature..."

TNC: *The problem seems to be at two levels: the local and the global. Taking the local first, how can local people regain control of their economies and create the economies they want in their own regions?*

Susan Meeker-Lowry: I think there are different ways you can do it, depending on who you are and what your local community resources and outreach are. Most people just get up in the morning, go to work, go to the grocery store, go home, watch the news and go to bed. For people who don't see themselves as entrepreneurs, or as especially creative, I would think that asking different kinds of questions about the company that they work for is important, finding out what that corporation or company does in the community, getting together with workers to address issues like values and lifestyle, recycling, and the specifics of what can be done so that people can start to know each other again— starting to build community on a social and cultural level. From that, you can start talking about economic alternatives.

TNC: *I believe that in Maine, at the moment, you're working on a sustainable forestry program that deals with the inherent problem of land ownership. Can you talk about this?*

Susan Meeker-Lowry: It's in the very beginning stages. The project grew out of the Northern Forest Land Study that was commissioned by the Forest Service and Congress to look at what is happening to the northern forests in Maine, New Hampshire, Vermont, and the northern Adirondaks in northern New York state. As a result of this study—which basically supports land easements, tax subsidies and that kind of thing— what we are proposing to do is to develop a bioregional economic plan for the region that would address issues likes jobs, creative opportunities, education, and resource use. Especially in Maine, which I think is 80 per cent owned by large paper companies like Champion International, International Paper Company and others, the problem is how to get the land out of corporate hands and into the hands of the community.

TNC: *Is that in the hands of the community as opposed to individuals?*

Susan Meeker-Lowry: Yes. I see that land really needs to be held by the community, because all people (and the other species) who live in the community are the ones who know the land best, and who know what their needs are. They don't have to worry about competing with Japan. They need to worry about whether their people have jobs, but they don't have to worry about high profits for stockholders. One of the strategies that we're proposing is to put the land into some kind of forest land trust that the E.F. Schumacher Society came up with in the 70s, and see if we can revamp it, and propose it as a strategy that makes sense to the people in Maine.

Then we could look at the forest as a whole integrated ecosystem, in much the same way as we look at rainforest preservation: detail a buffer zone, and detail a sustainable plan for logging and replanting—sustainable in the real sense of the word, not the way the corporations talk. The majority of the forest can remain untouched.

TNC: *Small businesses often face the problem of being unable to compete in markets dominated by high mechanization and cheap, exploited labour. What strategies exist to overcome these obstacles?*

Susan Meeker-Lowry: Perhaps the most powerful strategy available to us right now is people making choices in their daily lives to support small businesses over the other, corporate, mass-production businesses, even if their products cost more. If we continue to make all of our choices in the supermarket based on the lowest price, we will continue to support the corporations that we say we're working against. If it means we have to buy less, because we spend more for what we *do* buy, we need to be prepared for that, even those of us without much money. There are no easy answers on this one.

TNC: *At a broader, global, level, how can people have an effect on large corporations in order to influence the global economy towards being more ecologically responsible?*

Susan Meeker-Lowry: We've got to hit them everywhere, basically, with international policy changes that would come out of large institutions like the International Monetary Fund, the World Bank, the United Nations, and also legislative changes on state-wide and federal levels; investors need to be aware of who is doing what and they need to be able to feel good about making choices about what they do with their investment dollars based on what their ethical values are, rather than simply on a fat bottom line basis; consumers need to be aware of who is making what so that they can make good choices and then communicate the reasons for not supporting particular companies—by writing letters, for example, and letting them know that choices are being made on social and ecological grounds. We also need direct action to draw attention to corporate headquarters and to specific people within those corporations who are responsible for making poor decisions. We need to attack the problem at many different levels and on a massive scale. Not everyone is going to be comfortable dealing with all those different levels, but each of us can probably choose one or two to act upon.

"...if we continue to make all of our choices in the supermarket based on the lowest price, we will continue to support the corporations that we say we're working against. If it means we have to buy less because we spend more for what we *do* buy, we need to be prepared for that, even those of us without much money."

TNC: *Can you give us an example of socially responsible investing?*

Susan Meeker-Lowry: The easiest example to give is that of investors who rallied against South African apartheid by removing their money—divesting—from companies which operated in South Africa. Thanks to this issue, everybody then got to know what divestment and apartheid was. This was when socially responsible investment was just beginning.

Another major issue that investors have traditionally been concerned about is the production of nuclear weapons. People and organizations have just said "no" to investing in companies like General Electric which are making nuclear weapons.

Supposedly now the environment is a social investor's major concern.

TNC: *What about consumer boycotts: do you know of any examples that have worked?*

Susan Meeker-Lowry: Some that I know have worked for a short time include the Nestlé boycott for example, organized by InFact. Nestlé was selling infant milk formula aggressively in the Third World, and this was leading to a great deal of malnutrition—beause formula is not as good as mother's milk—and disease—because poor people don't have the necessary resources to keep baby bottles clean. The boycott forced them to clean up their act, then it was called off, and now it's back on again. Now InFact is boycotting General Electric because GE is one of the largest nuclear weapons contractors in the world, is very influential, and makes lots of consumer products, too.

Another boycott that supposedly had success was Rainforest Action's boycott of Burger King to protest the importing of Costa Rican beef. Burger King was involved in the destruction of tropical rainforest there, clearcutting the forest to make beef pasture for American hamburgers.

TNC: *Do you think boycotts work to actually stop corporations, or make them more ecologically responsible in some ways?*

Susan Meeker-Lowry: Sometimes I think they force corporations to change, and sometimes I think that their main advantage is as an educational tool, educating the general public around a certain issue. The Nestlé boycott didn't just educate people about Nestlé, it educated people about poor women and children in the third world. The boycott on Burger King educated people about what was happening in the rainforests and our role in that. As far as the GE boycott goes, that's a real hard one, because I don't know that it's educating anyone about anything except that there are very few alternatives to GE if you want to buy light bulbs....

TNC: *What about issues like the global rainforest destruction: what we can do locally?*

Susan Meeker-Lowry: There are lots of simple things we can do, like recycling, using recycled paper, so that we aren't dependent on pulp coming out of the rainforest. One of the best things we can do in North America is to set a positive example. We keep telling Brazil that they can't cut down their rainforest, yet look at what we're doing to our rainforests in the northwest! Ours are going to be gone in less than ten years; they've got a few more years than that before theirs will be gone. We really need to become much more bioregionally focussed, to realize that when we're acting to save our forests at home and educating people around that, then we are helping to save the rainforest elsewhere.

"One of the best things we can do in North America is to set a positive example. We keep telling Brazil that they can't cut down their rainforest, yet look at what we're doing to our rainforests in the northwest! Ours are going to be gone in less than ten years; they've got a few more years than that before theirs will be gone."

TNC: *Lack of access to working capital, especially for poor people, often inhibits the starting of new businesses. In Bangladesh, the Grameen Bank has been very successful in loaning small amounts of money to poor people with little or no collateral. Are there similar institutions in the so-called First World?*

Susan Meeker-Lowry: Not exactly. But there are things that are parallel, such as revolving loan funds. Now the majority of revolving loan funds exist for the purpose of funding housing or land trusts. The reason is because, obviously, the house or the land acts as collateral. It's harder to evaluate a business, you need a lot of expertise. Not too many revolving loans exist for developing businesses, but there are some. There's a program called SHARE—Self-Help Association for A Regional Economy—in Great Barrington, Massachusetts, which is a loan collateralization program that operates in conjunction with Great Barrington Savings and Loan. I see that the revolving loan fund can and will in the future expand to support worker-owned and co-operative business developments.

TNC: *What other Third and Fourth World examples do you know of that we here might learn from?*

Susan Meeker-Lowry: There's Sarvodaya in Sri Lanka which was actually a grassroots movement for community-based development. Trainers would go into communities and work with the people—especially women—to implement projects that they may have been wanting to do for a long time. This is really important in a culture where women have traditionally not been in those kinds of roles. They've been incredibly successful, involving many villages.

TNC: *In the final analysis, the distortions of national and international economies are rooted in the problems of money and value. Currencies, for example, are centrally controlled. There have been a number of attempts to provide local alternatives such as the green dollar system used by LETS (the Local Exchange Trading System). How do these systems work and how successful have they been?*

Susan Meeker-Lowry: The most successful alternative currencies were during the Depression when communities would issue scrip locally. The LETSystem has been successful in the past. It's a network of people with various skills. If you're a plumber and I'm a dentist, and you need your teeth fixed but I don't need my pipes fixed, in a traditional barter system we couldn't work anything out. With the LETSystem, you get your teeth fixed and I say that's forty dollars worth of work; so you are in debt to the system for forty dollars and I am credited in the system forty dollars—*green* dollars. I can take my credit and go to anyone else in the network, and you can pay your debt off by doing something for anyone else in the network. There is a community of members.

Now, however, in British Columbia's Comox Valley, where LETS originally started in an economically depressed time, it is losing ground because times are not so depressed. One of the questions I'm wondering about LETS is why it seems to work only when times are bad? It may just be that, when you've got money, you may just go to the hardware store to find someone who can do the job. I'd really like people to begin valuing the community for its own sake so that, even in good times, the community is worth more than the convenience. But we've got a long way to go before people think that way.

TNC: *Are there any community economic systems in your area?*

Susan Meeker-Lowry: One is called Farm Preserve Notes—a system set up to support two farms in the area. People will spend eight dollars for a ten dollar note and then, in the spring or summer, they will take that note and buy plants or produce from either farm. Because there's an actual physical piece of paper, other people can trade these dollars in exchange for cash. This is getting people used to the idea of a community-based currency.

TNC: *Even green dollar systems still use a money equivalent. Perhaps ideally, communities that are very close-knit could do away with money and operate on a caring ethic with the welfare of the whole community at heart. Do you know of any examples?*

Susan Meeker-Lowry: Not in this culture! Indigenous cultures have operated this way, but not us!

TNC: *Diversity seems to be the rule for bioregional economies. Presumably there are as many economic strategies as there are different ecosystems. How do you recommend people go about devising an economic strategy for their bioregion?*

Susan Meeker-Lowry: Well, they need to know where they live, and who's there as far as the human members go. They need to learn about the history of the place and how indigenous people typically "made a living" in the past, before European settlers came. We need to know what resources we have and what their condition is. Are the waterways polluted? What needs to be done to take maximum advantage without exploiting? We need to call a lot of town meetings to find out from people what they like about the community today and what they don't like. Then we need to devise strategies. In some cases we will have the necessary tools, in other cases we will have to invent them. One of the things we're all going to need a lot of is patience, because what we're trying to do is create an economy as if the Earth really mattered. Bioregional strategies will not necessarily be able to offer jobs like IBM can. We have to look at longer term strategies with more spiritual, natural and community kinds of rewards.

TNC: *In today's world that seems a difficult prospect. What do you think the chances are of people choosing a lifestyle change and the future of the planet over the immediate prospect of jobs and money?*

Susan Meeker-Lowry: I think that the chances are getting better every day because the Earth is speaking very loudly. I believe that more and more people are aware that if we don't start changing things today we will not have that option in five or six years—it will be too late. People don't want to hear this, they want to run away. But if we can be there at every turn, saying, "there is no escape," forcing people to face reality, and then work with them in the community to give them hope.... We have to do it—we've all got kids. We have to believe it's possible to change.

"The most effective way we can prevent power from corrupting so-called Green representatives is by keeping them at home, number one, and creating another power in opposition to the ever-centralizing nation state: that is the power of people in confederations of communities."

14

Cities, Councils
And Confederations
Murray Bookchin

T he way in which we view nature, and the degree to which we participate
in the decisions that affect our lives, both affect the quality of our cultures,
and are inter-connected. The "dominant paradigm" of the West sees nature as
primarily cruel and competitive which, in turn, justifies a view of human nature
as inherently the same. This, subsequently, has helped to determine our political
structures: hierarchy is the order of the day, with minimal opportunity for
co-operation and mutual aid—the major operating principles of the natural
world.

Murray Bookchin has spent much of his life thinking and writing about these
twin topics, his works including Toward An Ecological Society (Black Rose,
1980) and The Modern Crisis (New Society Publishers, 1987), to name just
two. As a historian, much of his effort has gone into a study of political structures
through time, and attempts to improve upon them, including the French and
American revolutions, and the whole anarchist tradition. From this basis, he has
also put considerable activist energy into the design of possible future decision-
making systems that would be of benefit to both people and planet. His contribution to imagining how the politics of a bioregional future might be—especially
in towns and cities—is especially valuable.

The New Catalyst: The modern crisis of industrial society is today being
described more and more as primarily an environmental crisis. What is your
view of the state we find ourselves in at the start of the 1990s?

Murray Bookchin: I think the environmental crisis is the most ex-
plosive example of our social crisis. In other words, I don't think you can

separate environmental from social, or spiritual, for that matter. We are literally undermining the natural world from which we emerged as animals. Over billions of years, we've seen the evolution of extremely complex life-forms and ecosystems; humankind is now simplifying all that. Humans have begun to create a kind of second nature (I'm using the words of the great Greek orator and philosopher, Cicero) that is now enveloping, absorbing and, to a great extent, destroying "first nature:" the wild, biological world from which we emerged. This second nature is our cultural nature—primarily social.

"There is a need for a new sensibility, a new feeling of care and of love for all forms of life, a feeling of responsibility, a feeling of atunement with the natural world that we are destroying today. It's terribly important that every environmental issue be examined in the light of its social causes."

TNC: *What are the main contributing factors, then, in humanity's creation of culture that are contributing to this, because we haven't always been destructive in our cultures?*

Murray Bookchin: That's very true, and that's been one of the central themes of my work. We have emerged out of a very co-operative type of society in which men and women complemented each other, in which people lived in small communities co-operatively, doing little or no damage to the world and, if they did damage, it was of only a local kind. We have developed a hierarchical world which didn't exist originally. The earliest forms the hierarchical world took were the rule of the elders—we still have this in our word "alderman"—and the famous Council of Elders that we think of when we speak of aboriginal or native societies. With that system, we began to witness forms of domination: the old dominating the young; then men dominating women, and men dominating men. Gradually this developed into a very elaborate hierarchical and, finally, class society, based on exploitation as much as on domination, and the nation state of which we are now the victims as well as the heirs.

This second nature—which could have taken such a richly co-operative form using our technologies, our intelligence, our capacity to form institutions, to design things—this second nature is now the biggest environmental problem we have! Today there's no wilderness left. Back in the '30s, '40s and '50s, I used to spend much of my free time in the forest, so I empathise completely with the Earth First! people who are trying to protect what is left of these early forests and other forms of life.

TNC: *So when people call it an environmental crisis, is that, in your view, a superficial analysis?*

Murray Bookchin: I don't think it's superficial in the sense that at least people are aware of the crisis. In 1952, people weren't even aware of what "environment" really meant, except in the most personal sense—if you spoke of their workplace environment, or their home environment. They didn't think of the outer world that much as an environment, least of all did they know what the word "ecology" meant. Now people are aware of the fact that there is an environmental crisis, and I support every movement that is trying in one way or another to abate it. But I think it is very important that people see the root causes, not just the symptomatic effects, of what is a tremendous social crisis, a perverted development of this second nature called society, and *analyse* society.

TNC: *Do you see the work to be done as much in our social and political structures as anything else?*

Murray Bookchin: Yes. There is a need for a new sensibility, a new feeling of care and of love for all forms of life, a feeling of responsibility, a feeling of atunement with the natural world that we are destroying today. It's terribly important that every environmental issue be examined in the light of its social causes. But I think, too, that this involves a spiritual revolution in our outlook toward each other and toward the natural world. We need a sense of our place in the natural world such that we, as products of nature, act in the service of natural evolution as well as social evolution.

TNC: *Your term, I believe, is "social ecology," seeing nature as inherently co-operative as the key. How do you think that viewing the world that way changes our actions in the world?*

Murray Bookchin: Well I think it makes it encumbent on us to function co-operatively as well. We must stop looking at nature as being "stingy, cruel, harsh and blind"—the traditional views of liberalism and Marxism and all the other "-isms" of the last century.

We don't know how to define nature. The early biological nature from which we emerged, along with other animals, was fecund, was creative, was rich—it was not simply a nature of "fang and claw" which is the way many Darwinians, and particularly Social Darwinians, have seen it. When one looks at nature that way, one begins to see that nature is not harsh or brutal or anything like that. Nature is riddled with co-operation, with animals interacting with each other in mutual attempts to survive. Those animals most fit to survive are those most fit to co- operate.

TNC: *Right. But that is not the view of modern society. How would you see* *trying to change that over-riding view of the world?*

Murray Bookchin: We need to re-educate people as well as we educate ourselves, to break with this mentality of first nature as being blind, brutal and cruel, and justifying competition, rivalry and egotism—survival at all costs. That's the first step.

I think we also have to rearrange second nature profoundly. We've been on a warped turn for thousands of years, especially with the emergence of a kind of economic system where you either grow or you die—a competitive system. In the western world, we have prized the idea that progress is identified with competition, and we're also witnessing this emerging in China, as well as eastern Europe and the Soviet Union. That's devastating. We have developed a culture in which we've said that, to move ahead in history, to advance, the whole goal is above all to grow, grow, grow, grow, grow. If you don't grow, you die, because your rival will devour you. So that, now, the grow-or-die mentality is having disasterous ecological effects. It means cutting down the forests, turning them into pulp to preach a gospel of more consumption; it's making tawdry, cheap, rotten goods; it's being indifferent to the soil, trying to get as much out of it as possible, turning it into a chemical sponge rather than real earth; it's polluting air and water, in the name of industrial growth, with enormous effects as far as the climate and the ozone layer are concerned.

"...nature is not harsh or brutal or anything like that. Nature is riddled with co-operation, with animals interacting with each other in mutual attempts to survive. Those animals most fit to survive are those most fit to co-operate."

We now have to establish what I would call a new synthesis: "free nature"—not only biological nature and social nature, but a new synthesis of the two in which we create a co-operative, caring, loving, and creative society that participates in first nature, that enriches first nature, that creates richer and finer habitats in which we as animals ourselves bring those products of evolution—our intellect, our capacity to communicate, our capacity to design and to think—to the service both of biological nature and our social nature.

TNC: *There's been a growing realization that the same structures that have oppressed the Earth and humankind are those that especially oppressed women. How must these structures change in your view?*

Murray Bookchin: Very profoundly. Right in the cradle. Women are almost the exemplars of the vast systems of hierarchy and domination that have done so much damage in the world. I think this reveals that we are talking about deeper questions than just conflicts between economic interests. We're really talking about the need for a basic revolution (I know the word is unpopular today), a basic revolution in all human relationships. And women, in the best of cases, often point the way to the need for a more caring society.

TNC: *Yes, definitely. Another of your key ideas is what you've called municipal libertarianism: the full participation of local people in the governance of their daily lives. Since so large a proportion of people today live in the cities, this seems a very crucial step forward. What background in history do you see for this, and how might you see it working in the future?*

Murray Bookchin: There's a long history on the part of people living not simply in towns and villages, but even in large cities—capital cities, like Paris 200 years ago, in the early years of the French revolution—who tried to regain their autonomy from the nation state which has really been in existence for about 400 years. People on a local, grassroots level have lost most of their autonomy, their freedom, and have lost even their desire to get involved in politics because they don't feel they can do anything. Most of the power that was enjoyed by people on the local level has been grabbed by the centralized state. But people even in fairly sizable cities like Paris, which had nearly a million people during the French revolution back in 1793 (the heyday of the neighborhood movements in the French revolution), fought to regain that power from the nation state and to form confederations.

TNC: *Also, isn't there the example of the eastern states, Vermont especially?*

Murray Bookchin: Yes. Not only in Vermont and in the American revolution generally, but I would say right now even in eastern Europe, there is more and more a desire on the part of people to regain local control. This may take a perverted, very bloody form of nationalism, I'm sorry to say (good ideas often appear in various forms, one cannot guarantee what form they are going to take). But people *are* trying to regain their autonomy.

Right now, in Quebec, a new movement called Ecology Montreal has been formed, one of the main goals of which is to form neighborhood councils. In fact there are two groups now demanding that Montreal neighborhoods—they still have them—be based somewhat on assembly-type organisations, and that power be given to the neighborhoods in the form of councils. So that, when you're speaking of the city council, you're speaking of representatives directly from neighborhoods, who are subject to recall, who are mandated by the people whom they represent, and who are continually subject to surveillance by the people in regular town council meetings. These tendencies exist everywhere.

TNC: *This seems to me to be the way that Green politics really should begin: to build from the neighborhood and the city councils and whatever local forms of power can be gained. Is this the way you see it?*

Murray Bookchin: Exactly! And let me stress that I don't think you can do it in just one city, or one neighborhood. The most important thing is that the cities interact with each other to form a confederal system. The main challenge now is, first, to make people politically conscious of the fact that they *can* take over their city councils. Second, that they can change their charters. And, most important, that they can confederate. Here in Vermont, for example, the Greens advanced the view that we must establish neighborhood assemblies, link up all the town meetings in a given county, and let the county unit be the confederal basis for that area's communities. The more privileged or well-to-do towns would share their resources with those that are less economically well off, thereby creating a spirit of genuine mutualism—mutual aid—in which we will feel that by helping each other, we are helping ourselves as well.

"...there's a long tradition in New England and other parts of the United States, in which the town or the village is merely the nucleus for a much larger area, bringing the country and the town together.... Their interests are pooled very beautifully."

TNC: *One of the things I particularly like about your idea of municipal libertarianism is that it overcomes the traditional antipathy of town and country in what I believe you call the "township." Can you explain how you see that working to break down those barriers?*

Murray Bookchin: You should understand, first, that I define politics differently from the way most people do. For me, politics comes from the Greek word "polis" which meant people managing their own community, the Greek "city state" as it was mis-named (it was not that much of a state). People met at assemblies once every ten days, not only to take care of their own affairs, but to produce some of the most amazing products of civilization: economics, science, philosophy—you name it. They unleashed a great deal of energy.

Now, there's a long tradition in New England and other parts of the United States, in which the town or the village is merely the nucleus for a much larger area, bringing the country and the town together. When town meetings are held in any township, farmers may participate who may live a mile or two miles away, and they're as much a part of the town as the retailers, or artisans, or manufacturers and professionals who live semi-urban lives. So that the farmer and the ordinary workman are all in the same community. Their interests are pooled very beautifully. I've attended I don't know how many dozens of these town meetings and people really think as though they're one people. That creates a new sense of citizenship, something very beautiful, where people are not looking at everything from their own strict economic interests—although there are always those individuals who do.

TNC: *Do you see the day when cities could actually be ecologically sustainable through this method?*

Murray Bookchin: I think they'll have to be, because we just can't go on the way we're going. I was part of the Second World War era, and I remember a Germany that was nothing but debris. Within five years, once the energy and resources were collected, that whole Germany was literally re-made until you didn't find any more empty, or bombed out buildings. This was a stupendous task. So it can be done. We *can* decentralize our cities, we *can* use our land intelligently, ecologically, we *can* have people create new kinds of communities, we *can* bring—as I've seen in New York—gardens into the cities and create new open spaces where before you had nothing but junk and clutter.

TNC: *Is it a matter of political will, or education, or what?*

Murray Bookchin: I'm afraid it's first a matter of a political movement being organized that sticks to these ideas, and doesn't compromise on them. I've seen all too many Green groups, which are very well-intentioned, try to compromise on these ideas, and be "realistic."

TNC: *The Green parties of Europe especially have had impressive electoral success in several countries. What's your view of their ability to significantly change society?*

Murray Bookchin: Well, the hope would lie with the Greens if they could get their act together, to be very honest with you. But unfortunately there's a tendency for power to corrupt. In the case of the German Greens, there's been a tendency to move towards the nation state and parliamentarianism, and while they are certainly doing a great deal of good trying to clean up areas, they're again still dealing with the symptoms. They tend to rely too much on the vote. Parliamentarianism can not only be an effective way of changing things, it can also be very corruptive. That's one of the reasons why I'm such a strong advocate of libertarian municipalism—the further away you get from your so-called constituents who, in my opinion, should really be active citizens controlling you, then the more you tend to fall into the hands of power-brokers who are prone to all kinds of compromises. Such compromises have marked many of the Green groups in Europe.

This is one thing I'm desperately eager to avoid in the United States and North America. Municipal libertarianism is not only designed to decentralize political structures in the city, and ultimately the physical structures of the city as much as possible, but also to maintain control of the people who profess to represent others—their constituents. The most effective way we can prevent power from corrupting so-called Green representatives is by keeping them at home, number one, and creating another power in opposition to the ever-centralizing nation state: that is the power of people in confederations of communities.

"We *can* decentralize our cities, we *can* use our land intelligently, ecologically, we *can* have people create new kinds of communities..."

TNC: *This seems to be very close to the ideas of bioregionalism, which is essentially very decentralist. Do you see the two ideas being quite close?*

Murray Bookchin: I think they're very close. I would only modify bioregionalism by saying that what one would call a bioregion should include agricultural land, urban land, and so on. A true bioregion should be an "eco- region:" a combination of ecosystems.

TNC: *The Worldwatch Institute, among others, is calling the 1990s the "turn-around decade," the idea being that ecological destruction is so far advanced that if we don't act now, in the '90s, to significantly change humanity's impact on the Earth, it'll be too late. Do you think that the alternative movement can find the necessary synthesis and strength to effect a global turn-around?*

Murray Bookchin: I think that as the impacts become more deeply felt, the possibilities for gaining those strengths are very, very real. In one particular community, there's been such a vast increase in skin cancers which people are trying to account for and which some people are saying is due to the thinning out of the ozone layer, that ecological consciousness must of necessity increase. And, although I would hate to think that that would be the main source, my hope is that the deeper the crisis, the more people are likely to respond.

TNC: *Given that things ecologically will deteriorate, what would you see as the direction that the movement could best take?*

Murray Bookchin: Well, of course, I believe in a very multi-layered movement. I would not want to see people involved in direct action activities give up their work purely to engage in electioneering; nor people who are very oriented toward libertarian municipalism give up their work, either.

The most acute and focal issue that emerges today is for a new politics to emerge, and that new politics is municipal libertarianism. It's not a question of going into the Democratic and Republican parties and trying to climb up the ladder, or of following a charismatic leader. The real task involves a conscious local politics that is at once educational and far-seeing for a given community on the grassroots level, but also part of a national network—laying the basis for a confederal relationship when there is success. If that national network doesn't exist, then however noble a community may be in trying to follow sound ecological policy, it's going to be isolated, and will not be effective. I think it is necessary to create a genuine network throughout all of North America minimally, and learn from the lessons of the Greens in Europe—some of which are mistakes that we should absorb and discuss—to build a truly creative, socially-oriented, outlook and movement.

Further Reading

If you have enjoyed reading *Turtle Talk*, you will really want to read *HOME! A Bioregional Reader*, edited by Van Andruss, Christopher Plant, Judith Plant and Eleanor Wright—New Society Publishers, Spring 1990. This collection of the "classics" of bioregional thinking includes work by Peter Berg, Gary Snyder, Caroline Estes, Jim Dodge, Starhawk, Nancy & John Todd, Ernest Callenbach and Wendell Berry, with a Foreword by Stephanie Mills. Alive with fresh and hopeful ideas, the book's large format includes articles, poems, stories and graphics—each evoking or describing a different aspect of bioregionalism. The sections include: "What is Bioregionalism?", "Living in Place," "Nature, Culture & Community," "Reinhabitation & Restoration," and "Bioregional Organizing & Politics."

Books by writers included in *Turtle Talk* are available from NEW SOCIETY PUBLISHERS:
Murray Bookchin, **The Modern Crisis;**
Susan Meeker-Lowry, **Economics As If The Earth Really Mattered: A** *Catalyst* **Guide To Socially Conscious Investing;**
Judith Plant, Ed., **Healing The Wounds: The Promise of Ecofeminism;**
Kirkpatrick Sale, **Dwellers In The Land: The Bioregional Vision;**
John Seed, (with Joanna Macy, Pat Fleming & Arne Naess), **Thinking Like A Mountain: Toward a Council of All Beings.**

In addition, the following books by other authors in *Turtle Talk* are available from The New Catalyst/New Society Books, Canada:
Peter Berg, Ed., **Reinhabiting A Separate Country: A Bioregional Anthology of Northern California;** and Peter Berg, Beryl Magilavy & Seth Zuckerman, **A Green City Program for San Francisco Bay Area Cities & Towns;**
Dave Foreman, **Ecodefense: A Field Guide to Monkeywrenching;**
Susan Griffin, **Woman & Nature: The Roaring Inside Her;**
Gary Snyder, **Real Work,** and **Axe Handles;**
Starhawk, **Dreaming The Dark: Magic, Sex & Politics;** and **Truth Or Dare: Encounters With Power, Authority & Mystery.**

Write for a catalogue to: NEW SOCIETY PUBLISHERS, Box 582, Santa Cruz, CA 95061-0582 (USA) or: Box 99, Lillooet, BC V0K 1V0 (Canada).